C000178468

THE TIMELESS
JAMES DEAN

THE TIMELESS
JAMES DEAN

by
Terry Cunningham
© 2004

Published by Stagedoor Publishing
B.M.Stagedoor London
WC1N 3XX UK

www.zoism.co.uk

ISBN 0 9521620 5 9

All rights reserved. No part of this publication may be copied, reproduced or transmitted by Internet or any other means without permission of the publisher. A catalogue record is available for this book from the British Library

Printed and typeset in the EEC

What is essential is invisible
to the eye – one sees only
with the heart!
James Dean's favourite quotation

All artwork © Mike Shaw

As an artist Mike has an international reputation as the foremost interpreter of classic movie scenes. His portraits of the famous in his instantly recognizable style are in demand worldwide. He lives and works in London

Acknowledgements
Thanks, friends. Without your help and support
Jimmy would never have lived again between
the covers of this book.

Joe Hosek (General Motors, Detroit); Arthur Bates (Porsche Autos, California); Diane Hanville (Arizona); Selina McCord (UK); The townsfolk of Fairmount; Natalie Wood; The Sheriff's Department (Paso Robles); the Winslow family; Warner Bros. Pictures; the Records Department of NBC, CBS and ABC TV; Arlene Grant; Moondog Miller; and to everyone who helped when the going was tough.

This book is dedicated
to movie fans young and old
throughout the world

Other publications by the same author include:

Travels on the Hound
South Across the River
The Great 78's
The President Demands Maximum Attack
Geronimo's Cadillac
Pacific Graveyard
14–18. The Final Word
Bram Stoker's Irving

Stagedoor Publishing would like to thank
Warner Bros. Pic/Corp. and the trustees of the Sanford Roth,
Roy Schatt and Dennis Stock collections for their kind
permission for the use of the photographs in this book.

Contents

Enjoy

I've been a publisher for many years and a Dean fan for even longer and just about every book that's out there about him I've read, and they must total about a hundred by now. Some were good but most were over the top Dean mania or character assassination garbage. Too many were devoted to the question was he gay? Who cares? (But for the record the author of this book tells me that in all his two years exhaustive research on Dean he found no evidence that he was.) Some years back when I first read Terry's book I thought he'd got it just right. So I asked him to update and revise it. As you read on I know you'll agree he give's us the perfect slant on a fascinating subject of our times.

In the 70's and 80's I lived in New York and went to many parties given by Andy Warhol, probably the most famous artist of the last century. These drug and booze induced gatherings were held at his huge studio called the "Factory". He had posters and paintings covering every wall. One group of portraits in brilliant colour made me stop and stare. Every famous face was there from Oscar Wilde to Liz Taylor, from Marilyn to Dean. Andy told me the artist was Mike Shaw and seemed surprised I'd not heard of him. He comes from your city London and he won't leave it to come to NY and work with me, he added in that rather mournful voice of his. So I feel proud that Mike has agreed to stop painting the famous for a while to paint the portraits and movie scenes in this book reproduced here in black and white. No other artist in the world today captures the mood and feel of the great movie icons, especially Dean, the way Mike does. So for your pleasure I bring you a great story plus great art work, and for the first time a revealing interview by Maria Moretti that at last puts the record straight. Enjoy.

Robert Appleby
(MD Stagedoor)

The Longest Time

I first saw James Dean in *East of Eden* during the spring of 1956 and I was immediately mesmerised by the degree of identification between his screen persona and myself. Later that year on a beautiful July evening, I saw him in *Rebel without a Cause* and also heard Elvis Presley sing *Heartbreak Hotel,* both for the very first time! I had to wait for almost a year before I was able to see him in *Giant*, and when I did, I fell in love with his fur-lined hunting jacket. I saved the money from my paper round and bought one that I thought was just like it. To be honest it wasn't but it pleased me for the longest time. Since then I've painted almost all the great names of screen and stage but it was James Dean who inspired me to become an artist.

Sometimes, just for a moment I would like to be there with Jimmy, making daisy chains for Julie Harris, or returning Natalie Wood's lost compact, with a playful wink; or even preparing an adoring pot of tea for a young and beautiful Elizabeth Taylor. When I paint my portraits of Jimmy, I can almost imagine that I am sixteen years old again and the world is a less complicated place, where it is always spring time where the good guy's always wear white hat's and where greed is not considered to be a virtue. I realise that dreams can only ever be dreams but maybe we should dare to dream some of the time.

Mike Shaw
(artist)

He's Timeless

It will soon be fifty years since James Dean was killed in a road accident. Yet his image and strange talent are as bright as ever. He is now the cult figure of all time. A Japanese PR Company recently carried out a worldwide survey to find the ten most instantly recognisable faces on earth. Along with such diverse characters as Micky Mouse and Princess Diana, James Dean was one of the ten. And he was one of the ten when they did the same survey fifteen years ago but in that survey the other nine were different and are now mostly forgotton. I'm willing to bet he'll be in the next survey they do in fifteen years time! All the others listed have immense wealth and power or have lived a lifetime in the public eye. Even the beloved mouse has the Disney Corporation behind him. But Dean was a poor New York actor who went to Hollywood and made only three films and was dead at twenty four, and has no one keeping his face in the public eye. Over the years various groups have tried to hi-jack his image for their cause but they fade into history and Dean goes ever onward becoming even more futuristic. In the interceding years since I wrote my first book nothing has changed. Jim was a star of the 1950's yet unlike most star personalities he's not locked into a particular decade – he's timeless. On screen he portrays a remote lonely insecure presence – qualities that are known to most of us. Maybe that's the answer to why he has held the interest and affection of a worldwide audience for over fifty years.

Terry Cunningham
(author)

THE TIMELESS

JAMES DEAN

Chapter I

The Early Years

James Dean is now a cult figure of enormous interest to a generation that was not born until years after his strange death. True to say other great talents of the entertainment world who also died young are still admired greatly. One thinks of Elvis Presley or John Lennon, but they were at the top for many years, turning out a string of films and hundreds of records that their fans can still enjoy. They were stars of the 1960s and 1970s, Jimmy's time of fame was the early- and mid-50s and he only starred in three films, yet today videos of those films are in tremendous demand worldwide, nowhere more so than Japan where his films stay in the top 100 year after year. Bookstalls carry magazines about him, every year people from all over the world make the trip to Fairmount, Indiana as I did to see where he grew up.

What was there in this young man's looks and personality that the passing of time does not relegate him to a mere curiosity? Jimmy's world of the early 50s was utterly and totally different from today's in just about every sense. In fact his mannerisms and appearance would look more at home today than they did then. Was he way ahead of his time or did he largely help to create today's images? Did he model himself on anyone? Who or what were the greatest influences on him, so helping to mould this strange being who has had such a direct effect on youth in the twentieth century? Let's try and find out.

In my opinion the major and formative influence was his mother, Mildred. A quiet and gentle woman who loved her only child very deeply. Jimmy lost that love when he was nine years old. Not only did he loose a mother's love, but a young mother – she was only 29 when she died in 1940. One now elderly lady, Mrs Arlene Grant, who I tracked down in Marion, remembers her well. She described her to me as a very pretty, rather plump girl with dark hair and lovely eyes, her maiden name was Wilson and her grandmother was a native American. She came from very poor farming folk and made ends meet by taking any job, waitress, factory worker, etc. but despite a lack of education she loved to read, especially British authors and poets of the last century; people like Dickens, Byron, Keats, Shelley. And like just about the entire population in those pre-TV days she spent at least three evenings per week at the cinema. She married Winton Dean at the age of 19, many of her friends at that time wondered why. He was a quiet type, but had nothing like her personality and lacked any spark or humour.

Jimmy was born in Marion, Indiana on February 8th, 1931. He was delivered at home and it was a difficult birth, when things started to go wrong Winton was panic-stricken and ran for the doctor, but after about half a mile realised he was running in the wrong direction. But like the movies of that time all turned out well for mother and baby. So grateful was Mildred that she named the baby after the doctor, who, although late, had saved the day. The doctor's name was James Emmick. Byron was chosen as Jimmy's middle name in honour of her favourite poet.

Jimmy spent his first four years in Marion, a town 45 miles north of Indianapolis, in the Green Gables Apartments on East Fourth Street.

Winton found it hard going on the wages of a dental technician, with a wife and a son, so moved in with a sister and her husband, Marcus and Ortense Winslow who had a farm in Fairmount, a small country town ten miles south of Marion. These were depression years for America's mid-West. Money was hard to come by; Winton was still struggling, but also still young. So he did as young men were often advised to do, he headed West and worked once more as a dental technician at the Sawtelle Veterans Hospital in Santa Monica, California. Mildred hated the idea of moving almost 3,000 miles away from her own family to whom she was close, and the area she had known all her life.

This was 1935. She had no way of knowing that the next time she journeyed back to Indiana would be five years later in a coffin. The marriage was not all that happy, Winton sombre and dull, Mildred devoting all her time and affection on young Jimmy. She had been taught piano by her mother and played moderately well herself, so Jimmy had to have lessons for not only piano, but violin, and would you believe, tap dancing. She also read aloud to him every evening, this way he got to know the works of all the great British and American writers and poets. They were, of course, living near Hollywood and the dream factory was working at full production during those years. Mildred was a film fanatic. One man who lived near the Deans admitted to me that he was attracted to Mildred and asked her for a date. The young woman, being very naive, said "sure" and turned up with a kid of about seven years old. The guy's voice was still full of exasperation all these years later as he recalled: "She wanted to see a Russian film that was showing at some out-of-the-way cinema across town".

We therefore assume that she lost more would-be lovers that way, but then Mildred was definitely a mother, not a lover. The film the old man complained about must have been one of Eisenstein's, the great Russian director. Jimmy recalled in later interviews seeing his films as a child, he also saw some great English films at that time when they got a limited showing, stateside.

Mildred even fixed up a little theatre in the garden where Jimmy and his young pals could act out little stories or even re-act films they had seen. Remember there would have been no TV to watch, so people made their own entertainment. Of course we can now see that she was over protective and even smothering the child, but our tiny hero was happy and felt safe and secure. He was to say in later life that he would have liked brothers or sisters, but that was not to be because Dr Emmick had warned Mildred at the time of Jimmy's birth that further pregnancies could be very dangerous for her, so all her love was lavished on one child and by all accounts the pair were great friends. An extra reason for Mildred's seemingly over-protective attitude was that Jimmy was not a strong child, although he became fit and athletic in his youth due to the outdoor life as a farm worker, but as a child he suffered bouts of heavy nose bleeds and internal bleeding, causing bruises to appear all over his body.

Early in 1938 Mildred gave up her part-time job as a hospital cleaner complaining that the work was too heavy for her and that she felt constantly tired. Money for the Deans did not prove to be any easier to come by in the West than it had been back East. The little house in Santa Monica was rented, Winton was driving a "32" Packard, payments spread over 12 months. Winton liked to have a drink with his friends, play some cards, maybe sometimes go racing. Mildred was happy to now spend all her time with her son. Later in '38 Mildred's cousin came West on business. In those days the train took the best part of a week to get there and he reported back in a letter to the family in Fairmount that Mildred did not look well and seemed tired and dispirited in her manner. She did not like the laid-back atmosphere and the nearly always warm and sunny climate of LA. She missed the changing seasons, the wind, the rain and the cold of Indiana. Her last years were not happy in California, she never really settled Winton was to admit later in an interview.

She did not bother to make friends or to get into the way of life out West, she was content that she had her son. The outside world, and its troubles, like the war clouds gathering in Europe, was of little or no interest to her and thus her tiredness grew worse. She also started losing weight fast and was constantly sick and most afternoons she would go to bed and rest, now it was Jimmy's turn to read to her. He was not an over-bright scholar, but he could read very well for his age and this he did, aloud, to his mother every day, all the stories and the poems she liked best. When looking back at that time later Jimmy was to say that he felt he gave his mother great pleasure by those readings, even though "I just knew she was asleep before I got through, then she would wake up and say 'I am listening Jimmy, I only had my eyes closed"'.

Her doctor advised hospital X-rays and the hospital, in turn, suggested her admission and a small exploratory operation. All this in the USA of the 1930s had to be paid for or you simply went without treatment. So poor Winton had to borrow heavily on insurance policies. The hospital diagnosis was as bad as it could be, Mildred had breast cancer, now she had to undergo radium treatment and another more extensive operation. Winton was beside himself with worry, he staked everything he had on this operation. He sold the Packard and most of the house furniture and even got an advance on holiday pay from his job. Father and son now made the evening visits to the hospital by bus and tram. "Those long trips by public transport were hell" , said Winton. Jimmy would say hardly a word, just look out of the bus window, but when he got to the hospital his face would come alive, so would Mildred's as they embraced.

Every visit he insisted on taking her a small gift, maybe some flowers or sweets, but always something. After the second operation the surgeon took Winton on one side and said, "I am so sorry Mr Dean, the situation is hopeless, your wife has no more than about six weeks to live". In the spring of 1940 Winton wrote and asked his mother, Emma, to come to Los Angeles to help them. This she did at once and could not believe the scene that greeted her in LA. Winton had gone to pieces, the house, half-empty of furniture, Jimmy off school (The Brentwood State) and Mildred, still looking so young and lovely, dying. Before she slipped into a coma she asked Emma to take care of Jimmy – "Promise me".

Emma and the rest of the family kept their promise for the rest of Jimmy's life, like the good Quaker people they are. Jimmy was in his ninth year when his mother died and Emma could see that her son could not cope with Jimmy, who now seemed to show a coldness, even a resentment towards his father. Winton was flat broke and heavily in debt. The Wilson family wanted their girl brought home for burial and offered to pay all the expenses, at the same time Emma suggested taking Jimmy home. He could live with his aunt and uncle Ortense (that was Winton's sister) and Marcus Winslow. They had a daughter, Joan, Jimmy's cousin, and a 400 acre farm in Fairmount.

Winton meanwhile could wrap things up in LA, get back on his feet and then return to Indiana in his own time. Winton, overwhelmed by grief and trouble agreed to this. Emma recalled Jimmy's sad farewell to his father on the station platform: "I thought they would have hugged each other, instead they just shook hands like two beaten-to-a-standstill fighters".

So began the long train journey back to Fairmount, the ornate coffin, paid for by the Wilson family, containing Mildred's body, locked in the goods section. Jimmy and his grandma up front near the engine. The character and personality of James Dean was now locked on a set path that would run for the rest of his life. The James Dean that the whole world would later know was now on that train heading East. While the body waited at the funeral parlour, Jimmy asked to see his mother once more and for a lock of her hair. These wishes were granted. He also took a ribbon from the wreath that bore his and Winton's name. Jimmy was to spend the next nine years in Fairmount and would see little more of his father, who, for the rest of Jimmy's life, would be no more than an acquaintance.

The Winslow farmhouse is a large 14 room building and has a rather isolated air about it. It stands on a rise looking across some 400 acres of rolling farmland, it was going to be a fine place to live for Jimmy. Here he would help his uncle on the land. It was hard work but he loved it, not many boys of his age had such a huge playground. He helped with the livestock and Uncle Marcus taught him to drive the tractor and to maintain it. For his tenth birthday he got his very own pony, but it was made clear to him that the animal's welfare was his responsibility. This taught him a love of animals that was to stay with him always.

When Jimmy was 12 the Winslows had another child, a son, Marcus junior. Their only other child, Joan, was now 14. It seems Ortense and Marcus went out of their way to show Jimmy he was not being pushed out. They bought him a small motor bike, he was too young to take it on the highway, but there was plenty of space on the farm to race around to his heart's content. He was now becoming healthier and therefore stronger and doing very well at the school sports. He fixed up a trapeze in the yard and smashed glasses were a regular by-product of this, also on one occasion smashed front teeth caused by hitting the barn door at great speed while trying to impress a girl friend. From then on his two front teeth were false. By his keep-fit training in the yard he became the school pole vault champion, also got in the basketball and baseball teams and did very well in the art classes and his greatest achievement of all, to his way of thinking, was when he was voted president of the Thespian Society.

This Society encouraged his love of recitation and acting. He would go out into the fields and speak or shout his lines aloud, his only audience were the trees and animals. An old inhabitant of Fairmount, who worked part-time on the farm in those days, Marcus had no full-time staff, told me he remembered seeing Jimmy standing in the middle of a field in the pouring rain, shouting and waving his arms about. "He made as good a scarecrow as ever I saw". The old timer continued: "I asked him why he did such wild things". Jimmy told him: "It teaches me to make my voice reach to the back of the theatre and also to overcome my fear of an audience". This fear of an audience, or even people in general, was never to leave him, not even when years later he appeared on the New York stage.

Although he was a successful student and also, now, in good health, except for poor eyesight, and in a home that was happy and full of love, from time to time, for no reason that those close to him could see, he would lapse into fits of depression and a sort of melancholy would come over him. Ortense asked a local Wesleyan Minister, the Rev. James De-Weerd, if he could help Jimmy. The Minister was a wordly 'man who had travelled much and had been highly decorated in the 1939/45 War for his bravery. He held the Purple Heart and the Silver Star and was just the sort of man who would hold young Jimmy's attention.

The two became good friends, De-Weerd said he soon realised that Jimmy was prone to self-pity and was obsessed by his mother and her tragic death. He would go over and over it time and time again like he was looking for some clue or reason that he had missed previously. From whatever angle he approached it the sad tale came out the same, this in turn sent Jimmy into even deeper despair. On one occasion, said De-Weerd, "I was up at the cemetery and came across Jimmy weeping at his mother's graveside, apparently it was the anniversary of her death, he was tidying the grave and was putting flowers on it. He asked me to stay and talk. And then for the next 15 minutes said nothing, until suddenly turning to me, he asked 'Do you think it was my fault she died so young?' I told him I did not, then he asked if I felt it could have been his father's fault. Once again I assured him that it was no one's fault. We were walking slowly towards the gates of the cemetery when Jimmy saw a frail old man trying to improve the over-run appearance of a loved one's grave. Jimmy wiped his eyes and pulled himself together than went over and offered to help the old guy who was pleased to accept. Jimmy stayed the rest of the afternoon with him and I will always remember that day because it sums up the James Dean that I knew and loved like a son".

One of De-Weerd's hobbies was motor racing, a somewhat unusual one for a Minister, but through him Jimmy became engrossed in the sport. They went together to Indianapolis to see the famous 500 race and to many other meetings. De-Weerd knew the drivers and officials so Jimmy was able to watch the behind-the-scene preparations, talk to the mechanics and meet the drivers from all over the world. Unable financially to own a car he contented himself with a tiny motor cycle that soon progressed to bigger and more powerful machines.

Today in Fairmount people recall a likeable young man who was into a lot of things and active in the community – a top sportsman, the basketball team relied on him heavily, his speed and skill saved the day match after match. At school he was now a leading light in the acting class, taking part in every production, either on stage or behind the scenes. Here, one of the teachers who specialised in drama, Adeline Nall, was a great help to him. She trained him in speech and dictation and remembers him as being very articulate and a very good conversationalist. "All that mumbling and stuttering he did on the screen must have been some sort of act", she said, "because he spoke nice and clear when I knew him, why he just had to, otherwise when he was on stage folks in the hall would never have known what was going on".

Around this time he dated a few girls, but around 1948 he became keen on one particular girl, now a shy, attractive middle-aged housewife still living near Fairmount. She remembers Jimmy with a wistful nostalgia. "He still holds a place in my heart and always will", she told me. "When he got his bigger motor cycle we would go out on it, just drives into the countryside, things like that, but I did not share his interest in motor racing, although I did help out with his theatre projects. The thing that stays with me strongly about him is the great love he had for the movies, he'd go every chance he got, usually alone. He would drive to nearby towns, even into Marion to catch some movie. He knew all about the actors and actresses and even the directors. He would discuss for hours the way a certain scene was shot. I remember two of his favourite stars were Robert Walker and John Garfield. When I see their films on the late, late TV show I can see Jimmy talking about them and impersonating them as if it were yesterday". As we sat talking in the cafeteria in Fairmount, for her the years seemed to roll away, as she recalled a very happy time of her life, "But you know", she recalled, "when with Jimmy I had always the feeling that you get when you see a bird in a cage, you want to open the cage door and say 'Fly Bird'.

Although I was too young to understand it at the time there was a great sadness about the boy-on account of his mother I guess. "I have brought this along to show you", she said, handing me a blue leather ladies' purse. Stamped inside were the words "Love always – J". "He gave me that when he left for California. He said he would send for me, but I told him "no", guess I must have been crazy but it was young love and to be honest with you it would not have stood the test of time. I could never have weathered the hard times that Jimmy had in New York. I go there sometimes with my husband on business and I hate the place". She asked me to promise not to reveal her name in print in exchange for so many personal reminiscenses. I agreed to respect her privacy and offered to sign a statement to that effect. "No need", she replied. "Just a handshake will do", she said with a gentle laugh. In that instance I knew why Jimmy had been so attracted to her.

She told me one of her own daughters was getting married that weekend and she asked me if I would like to go to the reception. I declined the offer as a I had to be moving on, but the very thought of her grown-up daughter brought home to me the distance in time of the events we had been discussing for the last hour or so. I walked her back to her car past their old school, she looked sad as she gazed across the street at the rather grim building. "Where the hell does it all go to", she asked, more to herself than to me. She closed the car door, the big engine sprang into life, the car moved forward a few inches then stopped, the electrically controlled window purred downward, "Hi, I'll tell you one more thing", she said smiling, "if any of those Hollywood people try and tell you he was gay take it from me they must have rocks in their heads". Then with a knowing wink she was gone.

He graduated from Fairmount High School in the late spring of 1949 with a medal for athletics and a prize for his work in the art class. In the nine years that he had been in the town he had acquired a love of acting and the stage in general, almost counterwise to this a love also of the outdoors and sport stemming from his work on the farm. He told Marcus and Ortense that it was time he took a look at new things.

He wanted to study acting in Los Angeles and Marcus told him the farm would always be there for him. "Why you're the best damn tractor driver I ever had", he told Jimmy, laughing. The family and friends held a farewell party for him, the party was reported in the local paper, The Fairmount News. He called on his old friend, the Rev. De-Weerd, they discussed motor racing, bull fighting, mystic religions and yoga. De-Weerd was an expert on the latter, he claimed it helped him with the pain of his war wounds. Just to end off the evening's conversation they discussed Winston Churchill, who De-Weerd had known during the war. Years later the Queen would invite De-Weerd to attend the great man's funeral in London. 'I wrote down a small text, or saying, for Jimmy to carry with him. I like to think he lived by it, it read: 'It's better to lose on your own terms than to win on anyone else's'."

He did not like the idea, or maybe the price of flying, so in June 1949 he boarded the big Silver Greyhound bus leaving Fairmount for the five-day journey to the West Coast.

Lucifer's Lost Disciple
© Mike Shaw

Cradle of Dreams
© Mike Shaw

Ladder of Dreams
© Mike Shaw

Steeped in Shadows
© Mike Shaw

Chapter II

From West to East

It was in a strange mood that Jimmy arrived in LA, it would appear that he had almost persuaded himself, subconsciously, that he was returning to a fairy-tale world of ten or more years previously, that maybe his mother was still there and that both her and dad would be there to meet him and all would be well now, and that happiness would once again be his.

Alas for him the mother that greeted him was a new one. Winton had married again in 1944, four years after Mildred died. Ethel gave her stepson a rather cool reception, Winton, second time around, tried to be close to his son, but due to his reserved and inarticulate nature failed again, dismally. He got off on the wrong foot by insisting that Jimmy studied law and enrolled him at the Santa Monica City College, whereas Jimmy's heart was set on studying drama and theatre arts at UCLA. He took part-time work as an athletic instructor at the nearby Military Academy, he, of course, joined an amateur dramatic group giving himself the rather romantic stage name of Byron James. The first production, a musical, was one hell of a flop, but unperturbed Jimmy began putting his heart and soul into the next project. At college he worked himself in as a radio announcer on the college broadcasting station.

Jean Owen was a drama teacher who helped produce the broadcast, she recalled Jimmy as very polite and shy and rather like Mildred his mother was before him, out of step with the West Coast way of life. She also spotted his talent for recitation. "He could recite, by heart, all the great poets" she said. "Once out of curiosity I asked him if he knew any Shakespeare, he went straight into Hamlet. It was just amazing. Here was this young, pensive sort of youth, peering short-sightedly at me through big horn-rimmed glasses, a typical mid-West farm boy, suddenly holding us all spell-bound with his eloquence and emotion. When he finished there was a long silence, then I and the other people present just started to applaud. I remember no one knew how to react or what to say, but a girl broke the spell by saying 'Jimmy, where on Earth did you learn that, did you get to study at England's Stratford-upon-Avon with Laurence Olivier and John Gielgud and all those English actors?' and at once Jimmy was himself again. Looking at his shoes and giving a little laugh, 'No', he replied, 'I practised for years in the middle of a wheat field in Indiana".

Jimmy's passion for the stage, plus his moods of depression, were already causing signs of stress with his new family. He and Ethel barely spoke and Winton found his role as peace-maker a difficult one, this time around Winton was a little better off for money so he bought his son a 10-year-old Chevrolet car, Jimmy was now mobile, "he had wheels" was his way of putting it. He could date the occasional girl, drive to the beach and watch the ocean rolling in, this he liked to do for hours at a time. He told friends he found it relaxing, but he had had enough of the cold, impersonal atmosphere at his father's place so to Winton's regret he moved into a rented room, taking the Chevvy with him, of course, claiming that without wheels he was "dead in this town". With his new-found freedom he felt he owed no allegiance to his father's wishes, so he quit the City College and enrolled at UCLA, but before the term started he decided on a quick trip home to the farm.

A friend of his, at that time, remembers him being quiet and withdrawn for some time, his explanation was that he was homesick. Suddenly he said, "I bet my uncle is having a tough time with the harvest without me there to help him. Guess maybe I will go back and give him a hand". The friend tried to persuade him not to make the journey in his old Chevrolet because the old crate would never make that distance, but it did, so one afternoon he turned up at his grandmother's. He told her that things were hard for him in California, but he was going to stick it out. Next day Marcus was out in the fields working like hell when Jimmy came into sight dressed in his old working clothes. All he said was "Hi, what job shall I start first?" That was a strange visit, Marcus recalled. "He told none of his friends he was back in town, he just worked from sun-up to sun-set with me, never said much, went on his motorcycle to Marion and tidied up his mother's grave. Also took in a movie while he was there. He arrived back in Fairmount with less than 30 dollars and he would not accept any money from us", Marcus recalled.

The film that Jimmy must have spent his last few dollars to see was Marlon Brando's first picture called "The Man". In this Brando plays the part of a paralysed soldier who goes through the film in a wheelchair. This was the first time a cinema audience had seen such a strange performance. Jimmy was fascinated and intrigued by Brando's style, his type of acting was totally different from all the other big name stars of the time. It was of course the Method School of Acting where the actor aims at getting right under the skin of the part so that he would know just how the person he was portraying would react in any situation. Later his own acting style would be compared with Brando's, but the general opinion seems to be that with close inspection he comes out as a very different type of actor than Brando, many think a far better one, but certainly having more sensitivity On screen he appears vulnerable, this makes the audience identify with him, Elia Kazan, the director, when discussing the differences between the two actors stated that Dean was far more refined in his acting than Brando and had he lived to make more films he would have surpassed Montgomery Clift, Rod Steiger, Marlon Brando and the whole works.

On his return to LA Jimmy teamed up with a young writer, Bill Bast, they were to remain friends for the rest of his short life. They shared an apartment – a tiny place on the top floor of a four-storey block, looking across the rooftops to the ocean. "We faced bankruptcy each month when the rent was due, but we loved the place", said Bill. "Our two girlfriends sometimes stayed for long weekends and we'd all pile into Jimmy's car, go for drives, somehow we'd find the money for the gas, we had some good times. I worked at CBS, the radio station, and got Jimmy a job as a car park attendant, he loved driving those big cars around, he was car mad at the time". Jimmy's girl was a UCLA classmate, Jeanetta Lewis, Bill's was a radio actress also working at CBS, Beverley Wills. Somewhere in the midst of distant time and sexual doublecross the story gets somewhat over-heated. It seems that randy Jim began paying Bill's girl some extra attention, they all found themselves in the apartment at different times due to them all working different shifts. It went something like this, Jim wanted Jan, but also if possible, Beverley, provided he could still be Bill's friend. Both girls wanted Jim, but Beverley also wanted Bill. Bill it seems wanted to get on with his writing, but liked all the other three. This was a pure dynamite situation that ended one sultry night in a punch-up, the two girls screaming like wild cats, Bill's typewriter got smashed a tragedy for any young writer, Jimmy nursing a black eye and crying with remorse, or maybe frustration at being found out and begging at the top of his voice for the three dearest people in his life to stay with him. But this show was over, Jimmy failed to win over this particular audience. The two girls and Bill packed their things and left, Jimmy now had to find the monthly rent unaided and keep the Chevvy rolling all on a car park attendant's wages, so within the month he was out of the apartment.

Around this time he landed the part of Malcolm in Shakespeare's Macbeth on stage at one of UCLA's big theatrical productions. By most reports he gave a creditable performance, but a few critics said, in so many words, that it was about the worst interpretation of the part since Shakespeare wrote it. A month later at last he got paid for acting his first professional job, a Coca-Cola commercial. It took two days to shoot and lasted one and a half minutes on screen. Jimmy got 10 dollars a day. A couple of weeks later the producer of the commercial was working on a TV play called "Hill No. I", remembered Jimmy and called him and offered him the part of John the Apostle, a very small part. Apparently Jimmy had looked very nervous, but one could see that the camera liked him, his vulnerable manner came across. The play was shown on Easter Sunday, 1951. This led to some small parts in films, this and the fact that he spent most of his time trying to get crowd work at the major studios, going for auditions and generally doing anything and everything that could possibly lead him to any type of acting work.

His first film was "Fixed Bayonets" – a Korean war film – in this he had just one line to say, then a Jerry Lewis comedy, and this time his dialogue was left on the cutting room floor, so he ends up just a face in a couple of scenes. After that his biggest part, to date, in "Has Anybody Seen My Gal?" In a bar he orders an unusual milkshake, saying, "I'll have a choc malt, heavy on the choc, plenty of milk, four spoons of malt, two scoops of vanilla ice cream, one mixed with the rest and one floating". He blew his lines three takes running and he said later, "Only an ice cream freak could get that load of garbage right first time".

But for someone with a burning desire to be a proper actor, Jimmy had to admit he was just marking time. He had made a friend of established actor James Whitmore who one day gave Jimmy a lecture on how to shape his career. Whitmore ran an acting class at UCLA and had noticed Jimmy's passion for the subject and his fanatical hard work in trying to do everything correctly, so he advised him to go to New York and try and break into the Broadway stage. This is where he would learn his craft. "It's time for sink-or-swim tactics, Jimmy". These words seemed to bring things together mentally for him, even socially he would never get off the ground in LA, he was not a sun worshipper, nor was he into beach parties, barbecues, surfing or swimming and the like, even his old car was not a convertible, He found the young crowd of the West Coast cliquey and snobbish with their affluent way of life. He also found them empty and the place a cultural wasteland. Some of his fellow students even bought their clothes from New York or London, admittedly with cheques signed by their fathers, but he still had the one sports coat he had brought with him from Fairmount. He appeared a lost and lonely kind of figure, even more so since he had broken up with the two girls and Bill Bast.

He got by, by shacking up with any pal who would let him share the rent for a few weeks. He threw in his place at UCLA, went and shook hands with Bill, phoned his father and called to say "goodbye" to Beverley. She described their parting, thus: 'I kissed him on the cheek, wished him well and watched him walk down the street. He kicked some stones, like a little boy scuffling down the street, then he pulled his coat collar against the night air, stopped to light a cigarette, turned the corner and was gone".

When Jimmy arrived in New York he was stunned and overawed and more than a little scared of the place. As a boy he made a trip with the school to Washington DC and one visit to Longmont Colorado in connection with a speech contest and of course he knew Los Angeles very well, but that would have been the sum total of his big city life. The sheer size and pace of this big city blew his mind. The huge buildings, the filth, the violence, the luxury, the wealth, he was used to one main street and this place had about 20. It was like ten cities in one. He arrived with around 40 dollars and he quickly realised that that would lead, pretty soon, to starvation, so for the first time he forgot his strong pride and wrote home for help, not to his father but the Rev. De-Weerd and the two people he called "mom and pop", Marcus and Ortense. By return they sent, altogether, 270 dollars and he got himself a room at the YMCA and replied to them that he would repay their kindness very soon. He seems to be saying "as soon as the big money comes rolling in".

He had a strange determination, almost a one-track mind or complete faith in his talent. It wasn't conceit, just a down-to-earth confidence that he would, one day, be a star, that some higher being had told him that it was all going to happen and to just hold on.

For the first couple of weeks he did not stray far from his room, spending most of his time at the 24-hour cinema show. Most days he saw at least two films. One letter that he wrote home at the time was very down-beat, he ended it with the words "Sorry to write you such a letter, but I am very lonely, so forgive me. I am just so lonely". One wonders why he did not head homeward to the farm and his girl, but we must assume that he was driven ever onward by his strange quest and obviously marched to the beat of his own drum. He found a small hotel room just off Times Square, it was even cheaper than the Y, but still the city overwhelmed him, he did not know how to get anywhere, or what bus to take, he seemed paralysed into inactivity. Finally he started on the painful round of producers' and agents' offices. He suffered the humiliation of snobbish office girls and self-important secretaries who kept him waiting hour after hour before finally brushing him off. On one occasion as he closed an office door he heard a secretary being sarcastic about his Indiana drawl, he turned and punched his fist through the glass panel and then calmly walked away, blood pouring from his fingers.

At last he landed something near to showbiz. There was at that time a big TV show called "Beat the Clock" where contestants have to perform some strange stunt in order to win large money prizes. Needless to say the stunts were almost impossible. Now to prove they could be done Jimmy, who was young and fit, was hired to do them during rehearsal. If he did not manage to perform them after about three tries they were dropped. He also took part-time work loading the trucks in a refrigeration plant and as a crew member of a New York harbour tug, anything to keep going. One day he got a letter from his old friend, the Rev. De-Weerd to say that a certain train pulling into Grand Central Station would have his old motor cycle on board. Jimmy was overjoyed, he now had wheels again, this would cut the expense of the subway, cabs or buses all over New York. Some days he would skip food, others he would be lucky to just have one meal and his weight was dropping and he started to look ill, not a helpful appearance when tramping around agents looking for acting work.

On his lonely rounds he met up with a young dancer in the same boat as himself, Elizabeth Sheridan, known to friends as "Dizzy". She remembers him as seeming very lost and intense, always wearing the same old raincoat over jeans, not the best attire for New York winters. Jimmy and Dizzy became inseparable. She formed a dance trio with two guys, Jimmy would sit in and help with rehearsals but work for all of them was hard to come by, inevitably they became lovers and moved into a small apartment on 72nd Street. The club act and her trio had folded and so far Jimmy had only landed two very small TV parts and once again the rent was due. It was now May 1952. His young friend Bill Bast arrived in New York, hoping to work as a writer for TV and Jimmy was delighted that his pal was back with him and the same day he and Dizzy were kicked out of the apartment for not coming up with the rent.

Then, almost re-living the LA situation, Jimmy, Dizzy and Bill found a small apartment on West 44th Street. Bill recalls, "We had to make a large down payment and all three of us were broke and though it broke his heart Jimmy sold his motor cycle. We were kids I guess, Jim would tell us about French painters who starved in Paris and only became famous after their deaths. Dizzy would wink at me when Jim wasn't looking and start saying she was only in the business because if you made it the pay was fantastic. This would make Jimmy mad and he'd say that all that matters was the art. She would continue by asking, 'You've just sold your motor cycle, right? Now, are you telling me you wouldn't prefer to have just bought a new Cadillac?' When Jimmy couldn't come up with an answer we'd all fall about laughing. But do you know now that I look back I believe Jimmy meant it, he really didn't have much interest in possessions or money".

The new apartment brought Jimmy some indirect luck. He was in an agent's office being given the "don't call us" routine and the agent was Lewis Shurr who was telling Jimmy that he should be taller and not to stoop, also glasses and a drawling accent were things that Clarke Gable didn't have. Jimmy pointed out that Gable was older than him. "That's another thing", Shurr added, "You are not ready for mature parts either". Shurr had an assistant, Jane Deacy, who was convinced Jimmy had something. She was about to start her own agency so she put Jimmy on the books and she stayed his agent for the rest of his life, guiding all his business moves. To this day she will not talk about Jimmy or give interviews. She went on to manage the careers of Telly Savalas, Steve McQueen and George C. Scott.

Another young actress on her very new books was a girl called Christine White. She got Chris and Jimmy to rehearse a little 15-minute drama that could be used as an audition to get into the Actor's Studio. They rehearsed for four weeks straight. The day of the audition came and Jimmy was so nervous that he knocked back a few brandies first and then ran around the block to burn off his adrenalin. Out of 150 entrants, Chris and Jimmy were put on the short list of 12. There was another audition the next day for the 12. Out of that 12 only Chris and Jimmy were chosen and he was over the moon with excitement.

But typical of Jimmy's life pattern he quickly became disenchanted with the whole set-up. Lee Strasberg, who ran the place, liked to openly criticise an actress's or actor's work and take their style to pieces. On one such occasion Jimmy stormed out in a terrible temper, never to return. He claimed the group had political motives, a subject that held no interest for Jim. He was correct in this accusation, but the real reason was that Jim probably did not like criticism and also whatever strange talent it was that Jim had he could easily lose at any school or in any sort of training or method. He would now try any approach to get work. He would phone people, write to them or just walk up to them and ask them.

Through Bill he heard about a producer called Lemuel Ayers who was putting on a play on Broadway called "See the jaguar", He called on the man and asked for an audition. Lemuel explained that they were not being held for some weeks but he would give him one, in the meantime he could offer him a couple of weeks work crewing his yacht, he was taking his wife and children, plus some friends down the coast for a trip. Jimmy took the job, he claimed later that he was seasick from start to finish but he impressed Lemuel with his hard work and pleasant manner and on his return he told Jim he would phone him when the audition time came around. That evening in the apartment Jimmy and Bill sat down to the usual watery soup prepared by Dizzy. "How would you two like some real home cooking he asked, "like steaks, roast beef, potatoes and pie and a couple of good night's sleep, no sound of honking sirens and heavy traffic, just the mooing of cattle?". "Sounds great, now eat your soup before you have any more hallucinations they replied. "I mean it", said Jimmy, "Come on, pack your things. I'm taking you two to Fairmount, we'll have some great food and rest, it'll be like a holiday". "Have you gone mad", said Dizzy, "What will we use for fare?" "Don't need it", said Jim, "We'll hitch-hike". "I remember thinking it must be around 900 miles", said Bill, "but I thought, Oh well we'll humour him, when he gets tired of not getting a lift, we'll be back here in no time". After three hours of not getting a lift Dizzy and Bill were crazy to give up, but Jim was in a strange mood, he kept saying, "Someone will stop for us any minute". And would you believe it, a well-known baseball player, Clyde McCullough, pulled over and just happened to be going all the way.

Bill recalls how happy everyone was to see Jimmy: "He showed us the farm, called on his old friend, the Rev. De-Weerd and we sure had the good food Jim promised, man, I've never eaten so well. We also slept in comfortable beds, the whole thing was so relaxing. Dizzy and I would have been willing to stay on as farm hands. I guess Jimmy saw that we were about all through in New York and just had to have a break from the harshness". But the spell was broken after a few days by a phone call from Jane Deacy, Jim's agent, saying that the play "See the Jaguar" was going to open sooner than expected and they wanted Jimmy for the part, so "Get back to New York quick". "I remember as we left', said Bill, "Jimmy saying 'Some day when I make it I am determined that they sell this place and move to a better, healthier climate where mom's arthritis won't bother her so much. I'll see to it they have the life they deserve, without all the work and worry that goes with a farm of this size"'.

"All too soon we were back on the highway waving our thumbs at passing traffic. Once more we were lucky, after a couple of short rides a guy pulled up and after a few miles he asked if we could drive. Jimmy said he could, 'Well, my ulcer is giving me hell, I don't feel too good so you take over, son' – the old guy fell asleep in the back and Jim drove all the way back to New York."

The play opened at the Cort Theatre, New York on December 3, 1952 with Arthur Kennedy as the star, but disaster for all concerned, it closed after six nights, a short run by any standards, but it got Jimmy noticed and a lot of work in TV plays followed and with them some healthy pay cheques. His first purchase was a brand new English motor cycle, a Triumph 500. He would tell people with pride that it was the same model the British speed cops rode. Sadly his lover Dizzy and his best pal, Bill, could not take Jimmy's new mild success. "He wanted to do everything for us, buy us presents, just keep us. Any bills we had he would pay", said Dizzy. "We were young and had our own careers and our pride and we couldn't handle it. Jimmy had our love, anyway, he didn't have to start buying it". So they split, Bill went back to LA to a writing job and Dizzy took a dancing engagement in Trinidad. Jimmy was alone again.

A TV crew member who knew him at that time told me, "The work and money coming in made no difference to him, he bought himself nothing except that motor cycle, after work he'd hang around for a drink with his fellow actors and the crew and then back to his room. Often at night he would walk the streets, spending long hours with a blind black street musician called Moondog. Many nights he would help Moondog by busking with him, the two singing in close harmony with Jim playing the bongo drums and at the end of the night he would check out the money, never taking any for himself, then see in the dawn with Moondog at some all-night hamburger stand. A strange way of life for an up-and-coming TV actor.

He was now getting a lot of TV work. The records I could obtain were by no means accurate, but it would appear that from May 1952 until making films took up all his time. He appeared in over 20 TV plays for NBC, ABC or CBS TV. He was sharing the leads with actors and actresses like Ronald Reagan, Eddie Albert, Mary Astor, Paul Lucas, Diana Lynn, Robert

Montgomery, etc. He always had a talent for drawing and he now spent a lot of his time alone drawing and painting, for the most part futuristic work that no one except Jimmy could understand. At one time he took his pictures around New York trying to sell them, but New York was not ready for his strange style. His fits of depression were getting out of control and as a fellow actor at the time said: "He was getting crazier and more neurotic by the hour".

In late 1953 he moved in with actress Barbara Glen. She was finding work only occasionally and was highly strung and temperamental so fights, sulks, then making up and becoming lovers all over again was the order of the day. But at least it took Jimmy away from the awful loneliness of walking the New York streets.

In January 1954 he got a break by getting a part in a play called "The Immortalist". Its stars were Geraldine Page and Louis Jourdan. This, for the most part, was an unhappy production. Jimmy would not conform or try to bring his unstable behaviour under control. He argued with members of the cast, turned up late for rehearsals, or not at all, insisted on driving his motor cycle through the stage door and parking it outside his dressing room. Geraldine said later, "I think the part he was playing, that of an Arab boy who was suspected of being homosexual, did not please him too much". It was a good part and he knew it, but he felt it was not what he really wanted. He knew a lot of young hopefuls around New York at the time, like Paul Newman and Steve McQueen, so maybe he would have preferred something more macho.

The play opened at the Royal Theatre in New York on February 1 1954. His interpretation of the part was, according to all concerned, superb – as a result he picked up the Daniel Blum Award for the Most Promising Personality of the Year but the neurotic behaviour continued, his live-in lady, Barbara, walked out on him stating loudly, "Enough is enough". Within three nights of the opening night he had a blazing row with the play's management and he quit, remaining only to work out his month's contract. During that time when not on stage he stayed in his dressing room, moody and unapproachable. One of his now few close friends was still his agent, Jane Deacy. She knew the director Elia Kazan who was in town looking for a new actor to play the part of Cal Trask in his next film *East of Eden*.

He tested half a dozen actors but finally narrowed it down to Paul Newman and Jimmy Dean. Jimmy being six years younger than Newman helped a lot of course and being a more sensitive actor, but Jimmy did not take it all very seriously, because he had heard that Montgomery Clift had been tested back in Hollywood. But Kazan got to know him and spent a lot of time with him, even to the hazardous extent of riding around on the back of Jimmy's motor cycle. He told Jimmy that he had the part and coached him every day for several weeks, right to the last detail of how he wanted it played. Jane Deacy sorted out the contract and in the spring of 1954 it was Hollywood time for Jim.

He prepared to make the journey on his motor bike, a distance of about 3000 miles. Kazan blew his top, ordered him to sell his bike and get on the plane, fear of flying or not. Maybe Kazan was the firm hand that Jimmy needed, his salary on completion of the film was to be 20,000 dollars. He kept repeating the figure to himself almost unable to believe it, his agent arranged an advance on his salary of 4,000 dollars. "When he landed at LA said Kazan, "Jimmy looked like a 'dead-beat' straight from the Bronx, complete with a parcel tied with string under his arm containing all his belongings. I had a studio car meet us at the airport and take us straight to the Warner Bros. studio where I had arranged that we had a small apartment-come-studio each. I wanted to keep an eye on Jimmy 24 hours day, you never knew what a guy like him would get up to especially with a cheque for 4,000 dollars in his pocket. The studio had too much money tied up in the production to have some unstable kid blow the whole works". Kazan need not have worried, at the last count "Eden" had made a profit of over 150 million dollars.

On one of his rare trips out on the town Jimmy looked up his pal Bill Bast. They went looking at motor cycles but it was only window-shopping because Warners had written into the contract that while making the picture motor cycle riding was definitely out. But not to be entirely beaten Jim bought an English MG Sports Car in bright red. Bast thought Jimmy was rather melancholy after not seeing him for some time. "I would have thought with all he had going for him he would have been more cheerful" he recalls. But as he got into the little open car, he said to Bill "Come on, let's drive, it will blow the cobwebs right out of our heads and man do I need that".

Shadows of Yesteryear
© Mike Shaw

Nightwatcher of Gethsemene
© Mike Shaw

One year old Jimmy with his Mum and Dad, Mildred and Winton.

The Winslow farmhouse where Jimmy grew up in Fairmount, Indiana.

John Garfield

Above and opposite: The two actors who had the strongest influence on Jimmy's acting style. In his youth he saw all their films. They both died young, Garfield age 39 and Walker age 32.

Robert Walker

His one-room flat, W.68 Street, New York.

Playing his beloved bongo drums with Moondog, his blind street singer friend,
New York 1952.

With Julie Harris in *East of Eden*

Talking with Nick Ray, director of *Rebel without a Cause* – a director he liked
and wanted to work with more in the future.

With Natalie Wood and Sal Mineo. All three became good friends
during the making of *Rebel*.

Playing bongos at his bachelor pad in Sherman Oaks, his first real home.

Showing a macabre sense of humour, posing in a coffin at a store in Fairmount.
Later the same store would arrange his funeral.

Cal: I'll keep it for you, I…I…I'll wrap it up. I'll just keep it in here and then you'll…

Father: I'll never take it! Son…I'd be happy if you'd give me something like…well…like your brother's given me. Something…honest and human and good. Don't be angry son. If you want to give me a present, give a good life.

That's something I could value. Cal! Cal!

The famous scene from *East of Eden* when he tries to give his father
(played by Raymond Massey) the money.

Looking uneasy in dinner jacket while attending a Premier with Pier Angeli.

With Elizabeth Taylor in *Giant*.

Nightclubbing with Ursula Andress.

Once again he shows a strange fascination for dying.

Jimmy in the new Porsche two days before his death.

BONNET LOCK
SCREENWASH
IGNITION & STARTER
WARNING LIGHTS
OIL IGNITION MAIN BEAM & INDICATORS
VENTILATOR
LIGHTS
MAP LIGHT
GLOVE LOCKER
WIPERS

CIGAR LIGHTER

FUEL COCK

CHOKE
HORN RING
HEAD LAMP SIGNALLING
INDICATORS
HANDBRAKE
VENTILATOR
DIPSWITCH
HEATER

R   1   3

PRESS DOWN

2   4

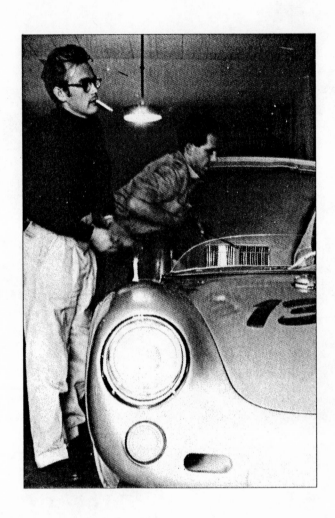

Jimmy with mechanic Rolf Wutherich, tuning up the Porsche on the morning of the fatal last drive to Salinas.

Technical details of the Porsche cars owned by James Dean

Speedster

Engine	(rear) 4cyl. opp.
Valves	ohv
Bore/stroke	74.5/74mm
Displacement	1,290cc
Compression ratio	6.5:1
Horsepower	44bhp at 4,220rpm
Top speed	90mph
List price	$2,995

Spyder

Engine	(rear) 4cyl. opp.
Valves	ohv
Bore/stroke	85/96mm
Displacement	1,498cc
Compression ratio	9.5:1
Horsepower	110bhp at 6,200rpm
Top speed	140mph

A last shot of Jimmy alive, driving "The Little Bastard", his nickname for the Porsche, with passenger Rolf. Photo taken from the Ford station wagon.

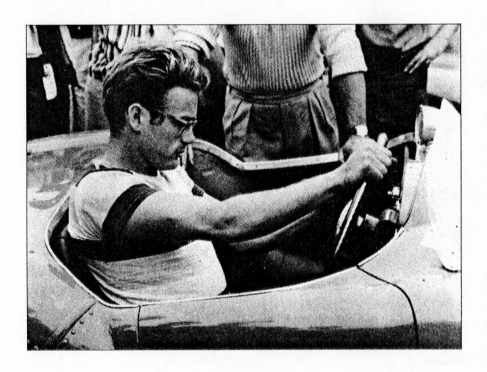

When Jimmy died they found among his few personal effects this photo and written on the back in his own handwriting was this poem.

Sound, sound the clarion, fill the fyfe,
throughout the sensual world proclaim,
one crowded hour of glorious life
is worth an age without a name.
By Thomas Mordaunt 1730–1809

Scene of crash.

Ambulance men prepare to lift Rolf (lying on ground), onto stretcher.
As can be seen, the Porsche just disintegrated.

Jimmy's body being carried to the ambulance.
Donald Turnupseed's Ford can be seen blocking the highway.

One Crowded Hour
© Mike Shaw

Crown of Thorns
© Mike Shaw

Chapter III

Hollywood

So Jimmy started work on his first major film, *East of Eden*, many would say the best of his three films. It's a story set in the Salinas Valley of California around 1918, Jimmy plays the younger of two motherless brothers, being brought up by their strict and religious father, played by Raymond Massey. Jimmy finds out that his mother is still alive and running a brothel in Monterey. He borrows money from her to help his father, whose farm is in trouble. He is constantly trying to win his father's love. After making some money of his own, with the help of his mother's loan, he tried to give the money to his father, only to be rejected, this scene is regarded by cinema buffs as one of the best in the history of film making. His brother's girlfriend, played by Julie Harris, also plays a big part in the scene. The overall effect is pure artistry.

Kazan said later that after doing that scene, "I realised that I was dealing with a talent that was pure gold. I said to him, Jimmy, people will be watching that long after we've gone and they'll still think it's great'. This seemed to please him tremendously". But for all his appreciation of the actor's skills

Kazan's personal feelings for Dean were to say the least becoming debatable. He was such a vulnerable sort of guy and was getting to be more and more paranoiac. One of his obsessions was that people of his own age in the film city at that time who had wealthy parents behind them were against him, so anyone who had come from money or was loaded anyway was no friend of his. This tag probably fitted 99% of the people he had to deal with on a daily basis, hence not too many friends.

His old New York rival, Paul Newman, was making his first film "The Silver Chalice" in Hollywood at the same time and introduced him to his co-star actress, Pier Angeli. They were attracted to each other at once and within a few weeks were enjoying a pleasant young love affair. They rented a very small cottage on the beach, well out of LA, and spent their free time in simple pursuits. Sun bathing on the beach, going to drive-in movies, Jimmy still had his passion for watching films so they spent many an evening at the cottage doing just that. They were, by all reports, very happy in each other's company.

Here one has to cut through the silly stories from fan magazines, publicity hand-outs, gossip and just plain lies. A lot of misleading nonsense was written about this romance, but speaking to people who knew the couple at the time it appears that as soon as the romance took hold the storm clouds began to gather. Pier and her actress twin sister were from a very strict Italian family, ruled over by Mama Angeli, they were also very strict Catholic. Young romeo Jimmy began talking of marriage and family and even more completely out of character he took the girl to meet his father and stepmother. Everything was sweetness and light until Pier's mother, who had stated already her dislike for Jimmy, suggested or even ordered that Jimmy would have to become a Catholic. Jimmy had been brought up a Quaker

But more important to a mentality like Jimmy's was the order "you must change, got to... etc" – this was a red rag to a bull indeed. He said to Bill Bast "Why the hell must I change, no bastard's telling me what to do. Everything I've done has been done on my own terms. I'll take orders from no one". Now Jimmy was right back in character; in love with Pier and very protective towards her because she had a weak heart and wanting to get married.

But totally unwilling to compromise or give ground or, as he saw it, back down. So he stormed back to New York to do a TV play. Pier sent him a note before he left telling him to take it easy in his new sports car – promise me, she adds as a PS – because it seems they had a very near-miss on Sunset Boulevard between Jimmy's MG and a bus. Pier's mother began to put pressure on her daughter to marry someone of Italian descent, she thought marriage to that American boy, Dean, would be a disaster. So poor Pier, who was quiet and gentle by nature, nor very strong physically, ended the romance. Within weeks she met and married recording star, Vic Damone.

The wedding was a big affair, even by Hollywood standards. The story goes that Jimmy waited outside the church on his motor cycle and as the bride and groom came out he revved up the machine and roared off down the road in some sort of defiant gesture. Out of all the eight guests at that wedding that I managed to trace, not one of them recalled seeing anyone outside on a motor cycle.

In fact on that day, November 24 1954, the documentary evidence is that he was way across town, writing out a cheque for a new Porsche Speedster, trading his MG in part payment. Pier's life and career took a strong downward turn from that time on. She divorced Vic Damone in 1958, then married another Italian musician, that lasted only two years, her film career collapsed, she could get no work at all and lived in extreme poverty getting by with odd jobs and hand-outs from family and friends. She died in 1971 from a drug overdose, according to the newspaper reports, but on closer inspection of hospital reports and records this was untrue. She died of her old complaint – heart trouble. Four months before her death she wrote a letter to an old actress friend. In it she stated "the only real love of my life was Jimmy Dean".

Before his next film Jimmy made one, and as it turned out last, trip back to Fairmount to his roots on the farm. He took with him Dennis Stock who was doing a photo series on this new star for Life magazine. "Somehow", said Dennis, "Jimmy acted as if it was the last time he would see the farm or his old home". It was a happy family reunion, Stock took photos of Jimmy on the farm walking around town, and with friends and family. A real strange incident he recalls was in town passing a funeral parlour. "That's the firm that arranged my mother's funeral", Jimmy told him. "With that", recalls Dennis, "He goes inside and gets into one of the coffins and gets me to take a picture, we were lucky to get out of there before the police arrived".

Rebel Without A Cause turned out to be a great film for Jimmy, still regarded today as a cult picture, the action takes place over 24 hours, Jimmy is on the screen the whole of that time. He carries the whole thing. Warner Brothers took advantage of this new star situation. "Rebel" was a cheap film to make, no big names to back up Jimmy, no big sets, the end result was it made a fortune. Only recently TV rights have been sold worldwide to make a second fortune. It's a story of a new boy at High School, isolated and alone, also unable to get close to his parents, he becomes friends with equally troubled loner, Sal Mineo and the girl next door, Natalie Wood. The school gang give them a bad time and inevitably Jim and the gang leader clash in a knife fight and later a chicken run in stolen cars driven fast to the edge of a cliff. The first driver to get out is a coward. In the run the gang leader is killed and it all ends in a deserted mansion. The mansion used is the late Paul Getty residence, where the lonely three are hiding.

The gang track them down and so do the police. Jimmy tries to save his new friend, but Sal Mineo is shot down by a trigger-happy policeman. The closing scenes show Jimmy at last getting together some sort of relationship with his parents and beginning we assume, a life-long, happy-ever-after romance with Natalie Wood. One gets the impression that Jimmy was happier making this film than he was making *East of Eden* or *Giant*. He got on well with all the cast, especially the director Nick Ray who said "It was a great picture to make. Jimmy was a very lonely guy, he'd hardly any friends in Hollywood and mistrusted everyone. But when he got to know me he relaxed a lot and we became great pals, I let him make suggestions about every scene and we all went around together after work, the whole team became close, sometimes I directed a scene and I'd think to myself 'that's not so good', but when I saw the same scene on the screen, he was superb, he just understood the camera. He was, without doubt, the greatest actor I ever worked with".

The two supporting parts in "Rebel" went to Natalie Wood and Sal Mineo, it was the start of their careers and after working with Dean they found their bargaining power increased dramatically. Sal was quoted as saying, "I never worked again with an actor like Jimmy, he didn't act a part, he lived it. He also went out of his way to help me, if I blew a scene he'd say, 'Don't worry, take it easy you'll get it this time'. He just never acted like a big star. I still miss him". Sal Mineo was murdered by muggers outside his Los Angeles apartment in 1976. Natalie Wood told me in a telephone interview, "Sometimes Jimmy wouldn't even hear you when you spoke to him, he would just switch off, he could concentrate totally, but he was always polite and nice to be with. At that time a lot of big people were snubbing him, maybe they were frightened of this startling new talent, that was so completely different from anything we knew at that time. If those people think their pools or their Cadillacs are threatened, they pull up the drawbridge and quickly.

"I remember he wanted Montgomery Clift to come to a party but Clift refused to have any dealings with Jimmy, mind you, he was having health problems at the time. I think he was awaiting an eye operation. Then he tried to contact Brando, he would have to leave a message on the answering machine, what Jimmy didn't know was that Brando was listening to him all the time and making fun of him. He should have Jimmy's talent or manners! I often wonder, if he had lived, what sort of movies he'd be making now. You can bet they'd be first class entertainment and that's the business we're in and Jimmy knew that better than most", she concluded. A few weeks after that interview Natalie died in a tragic drowning accident in California.

When he was introduced to other big stars at the studio, like Spencer Tracy, Clark Gable, Humphrey Bogart, the reception he got was, to put it mildly, cool except in the case of Gary Cooper. He tried to introduce him to Hollywood society. Cooper spent the day on the set chasing indians and drinking with cowboys, but after work he and his wife, Rocky, were great social entertainers giving parties for top people from all walks of life, medicine, law, politics at their mansion in West Los Angeles. He invited Jimmy to a white-tie affair one evening.

Jimmy made the effort only to get as far as the large stately front door opened by a butler, he took one look at the large gathering of very upperclass Hollywood guests talking quietly in deep conversation, broken only by the "clink" of cocktail glasses and he fled away into the night, never to return. He phoned Cooper the next day and said "Sorry, but I just couldn't make that scene, but thanks for asking me".

At the completion of "Rebel" he was exhausted, "Never has any acting job taken so much out of me, I put everything I had into that one and I am pleased with the general result. Any writer, musician, painter or actor will tell you that when they look back on their work they know it could be improved, but in the end you have to say 'OK that's it, it's finished, it stands or falls as it is'. I now regard Natalie, Nick and Sal not as co-workers, I regard them as friends, about the only friends I have in this town and I hope we all work together again soon".

Well, Sal worked with him again on *Giant*, but that was about it. Sadly at the time of writing they are all dead now. Nick Ray died of an overdose after being told he had terminal cancer, the other three died violently, long before their time.

Just three days after Nick Ray yelled "That's it, it's in the can" and the happy film crew, actors and everyone said their fond goodbyes, Jimmy once again packed his few bits and pieces and headed for a Texas town called Marfa, the population at that time under 3,000, situated in south-west Texas, almost on the Mexican border, therefore you get temperatures of 120 degrees in the shade. He arrived there on June 3 1955. He was in this rather God-forsaken place to start filming *Giant*. *Giant* was a film lasting over three hours, it deals with 30 years of Texas, that vast stretch of land that has always been the proudest state in America. It opens in 1923 when a strongwilled girl, Elizabeth Taylor, falls for a young Texan ranch owner, Rock Hudson, who visits her father's farm in Maryland to buy a horse and they return to Texas as man and wife.

After the green fields of home Elizabeth finds the eye-wearying bleakness of Texas almost unbearable, she is also appalled by the way the ranch is run and the dreadful conditions of the Mexican workers and servants. Against the wishes of her husband she sets up a medical centre, a young ranch hand, James Dean, is employed by them and inherits a small piece of land that later produces oil. As the years go by he makes millions, they quarrel and fight yet his love for Elizabeth remains constant. It is brilliantly photographed and very well acted, Jimmy plays the part of the ranch hand in a lonely, bitter, quarrelsome style. He has to age over 30 years during the course of the film, this he does far more effectively than Taylor or Hudson, whose only claim to age appears to be a slight greying of the temples.

At the end of the film Jimmy, real age 24, is playing a man in his late 50s, quite a feat for any actor. George Stevens, the director, was a quiet and friendly man, but on set all sign of that disappeared. He ran the whole show like an Army manoeuvre. He had a great track record for box office successes behind him, in fact his previous picture was "Shane" with Alan Ladd and jack Palance, just about the biggest hit film of the early 50s. Stevens also wanted Ladd for the part Jimmy was to play in *Giant*, but Ladd rejected it. The authoress, Edna Ferber, had agreed to take no salary for the novel that took her two years to write, but to have a 12% share of the profits during its first two years of life. Stevens and Warner Brothers were heavily mortgaged to the East Coast Banks for over 5 million dollars before one foot of film had been shot, so he could afford no artistic tantrums, but once again the name Dean on the posters helped to ensure success; in its first year of release it paid for itself making some 7 million dollars and stayed the biggest money maker Warner Brothers had until "My Fair Lady" came along ten years later.

Jimmy missed the closeness of working with Nick Ray, George Stevens worked in a very different style, he shot a scene from every possible angle. He had a reputation for shooting 65,000 feet of film for every 10,000 feet that ended up on the screen. Jimmy took no time at all to fall out with his fellow actors, Rock Hudson and Chil Wills, yet unexpectedly became friendly with Liz Taylor. They were about the same age and acted like brother and sister and she appeared to help him when the pressure got too much and to defend him against people like Stevens, in much the same way as the other two women in his film life, Julie Harris and Natalie Wood had done before her.

The filming ended and the cast went their separate ways, there was talk of Jimmy getting an Oscar for his performance. *Giant* has now become one of Hollywood's magnificent, rambling, great motion pictures. But Jimmy's own troubled nature was continuing to pull him down, he was seeing a lot of actress Ursula Andress. It was very much a physical attraction and looking at photos of Ursula at the time one can understand

Jimmy's train of thought, but the affair quickly died when he found out that she was the daughter of the German Consul in Berne and had spent her youth at one of Switzerland's finest finishing schools for girls. He remarked to a friend "What the hell would she have in common with a poor farm boy. If it weren't that I was up there on the screen, her and people like her wouldn't give me the time of day'.

One subject that was fast becoming a passion with him was motor racing, he'd been a devotee since the days back in Fairmont when the Rev. De-Weerd took him to see all the big races, but now he had the money coming in to indulge to the full in this expensive pastime. During the filming of *Giant*, director Stevens had banned him from any form of driving, even made him leave his Porsche back in Hollywood. He could not afford to risk one of his major `investments ending up in hospital. Before shooting began on *Giant* Jimmy had taken part in five race meetings, the first was an amateur meeting at Bakersfield. Some professional drivers also took part so the standard of driving was high and fast. He took part in four races that weekend and by all accounts drove well, winning three of the races, thereby collecting a couple of trophies.

He then entered two more meetings at Palm Springs and Santa Barbara. He displayed a total disregard for his own safety and drove like a bat out of hell. In one race he led all the way until the last lap when he was overtaken by a professional driver, Ken Miles, who claimed later, "If that guy gives up showbiz and studies racing, he's got the making of being as good as anyone in the USA or on the European tracks". In his last race he found himself up against more powerful cars, like jags and Corvettes. Driving flat out to hold his place on the straights, the engine of the Porsche blew up and he taxied to a stop, luckily in one piece. But now that he was back in Hollywood he was eager to start racing again.

He rented a small house in Sherman Oaks, a sort of converted lodge consisting of one large main room. His sole companion was a cat called Marcus that Liz Taylor had given him. Most evenings he would spend the time playing his bongo drums or listening to records, anything sooner than go out and face people. He had ideas about his next film, the studio suggested "Billy the Kid", but he was not at all keen on that. He'd been reading about First World War English poet, Rupert Brooke. The fact that Brooke was roaming around the South Seas in 1914, but headed straight home when he heard that his country was in trouble appealed to the romance in Jimmy, although he appeared to overlook the fact that Brooke was a well built six foot and a very English public schoolboy.

But his main burning desire was to play Hamlet, not in the usual style, he regarded Olivier and the like as too old. Shakespeare, he said intended Hamlet to be young, unsure of himself and confused. He made drawings of unusual sets and listed actors who were not thought of as Shakespearian to play alongside him. Whether the studios would have put up the money or not we will alas never know.

His agent, Jane Deacy, had arrived briefly in California to go over a new contract she had engineered for Jimmy. Although he was not a money person it nearly blew his mind, one million dollars for eight pictures spread over the next six years, with at least three months of each year off to do as he wished, TV work, the New York stage, car racing, or just travel. "When I had finished going through the details", said Jane, "he just started to cry. I asked him what was wrong and he told me that his depression was becoming so bad he was seeing an analyst, but it was not doing a lot of good. 'I've just no faith in the guy', said Jimmy, 'I'm being conned by this bum who is just taking my dough". "Then why waste any more time with it all", said Jane. "Let's go and celebrate, after all, when you have a bank account that stands at one million dollars you can afford to be crazy This made Jimmy laugh and we went out and met friends and had a good evening, but at one point in the evening Jimmy got serious, pulled me to one side and said, 'You know, Jane, with that much bread coming in I'd better make a Will', I said 'OK, I'll send someone over to fix it."

The one who came over within a day or so was Lou Bracker who was an accountant and in the insurance business. First Bracker drew up an insurance policy for 100,000 dollars, Jimmy told him "I want 80,000 to go to my aunt and uncle, Marcus and Ortense Winslow who raised me, but a separate 10,000 for my grandparents, Mr and Mrs Dean, also a separate 10,000 dollars put by for young Marky's education. That's it, simple, nothing for no one else". Bracker pointed out that the film earnings plus this policy would be distributed this way in the event of his death, but he had to make a formal Will to make it legal. "Jimmy seemed to avoid the issue", said Bracker, "Let's do it now Jim, I have the papers". "No, no", said Jim, "I'll sit down one evening next week and do it properly, a few days don't matter, I don't feel ill or anything". "I decided not to push him, maybe the making of a Will upset him like a lot of other people, so I said, 'OK, I'll call over next week'. I think somehow the making of a Will spoilt the effect of his new-found wealth".

But of course he never did make that Will, so when he died everything went to his next of kin, his father, Winton Dean, who was not even on the list of people that Jimmy had drawn up, but under Californian law if the deceased leaves no Will that's the way it is. Jane Deacy had worked out his schedule so that his next job was to be a TV play in New York, then the next year, 1956, he would have the whole year off. He stated that in that year he would devote himself to motor racing around the world. Where cars were concerned Jimmy was now going completely over the top, aided by his new wealthy status, with his liking for anything European he ordered an English Lotus Mark 8, due to arrive in the USA November 1955. He had put a deposit on another more powerful, but rare English car, a Bristol. This was for when he moved up to the bigger, more powerful races. Jimmy described it as "a British monster on wheels".

The next day after talking to Bracker he met Rolf Wutherich, on the street. Rolf was 28 years old and worked as a mechanic for Competition Motors where Jim had purchased his Porsche Speedster. "I remember said Rolf, "Jimmy seemed in a light-hearted mood and he had a toy monkey on his wrist that bounced up and down on elastic. Today a bit odd, but in 1955 really weird, man. He told me about his Lotus and Bristol coming from Europe and I told him about the new Porsche Spider that had just arrived at the showroom, he couldn't wait to see it so I took him around there. He fell for it at first sight and drove it twice around the block. I advised him to wait and think about it. After all he had two other great cars on the way, but no, he was obsessed, he wrote out a cheque there and then, the total cost of the car was 6,400 dollars, but we took his other Porsche in part exchange. He also insisted that I come with him to all race meetings and work on the car in the pits. Jimmy was to pay me a fee plus all my travel expenses. "I plan to become World Racing Champion", he told me and I think he meant it.

But the records show that this new car of Jimmy's was something very different and much more potent that anything he had known before. For example, it was made of extra lightweight aluminium that crumpled like paper in the crash, giving no protection whatsoever. It had no windscreen, no top and no bumpers or excess weight of any kind. Its colour was silver, the German racing colours, and it had a top speed of 140 miles per hour. It was made solely for track racing, it was simply a speed machine. He drove it around Hollywood showing it to his friends. One pal told me "It seemed to cheer him up, he was real proud of that car, he had to get 1,500 miles on the clock slowly, to run in the engine, but it sure got him out of the house and away from that lonely brooding he was into".

Jimmy heard that there was to be a big race meeting up at Salinas, a town some seven hours drive to the North of LA. He immediately phoned through his entry and booked himself a place. He contacted Rolf, his mechanic, who said he would be free to go and then in his excitement he began phoning everyone and anyone to go along with him, most were too tied up with their own work or were out of town. His old pal, Bill Bast, was working on a TV film (Bast had a complete breakdown after his friend's death). Nick Ray had just left for England on business, his aunt and uncle, who had just spent a week in town staying at Winton's, were returning to Fairmount.

So on Wednesday he set off with his friend Bill Hickman. Jim had met Hickman during the making of *Giant*. He was the drama coach on that film, also a film stunt man, mainly car chase stunts, he later did the driving in the film "The French Connection". He was also a racing fanatic. Rolf, the mechanic, would follow on later in his own car. They set out around 6 pm but by the time they got to Santa Barbara the fog was rolling in so thick they had no choice but to turn back. On the way back a highway patrol car dropped in behind Jimmy, but Hickman recalls Jimmy had put his foot down and "we just lost that patrol car. I remember Jimmy said, 'Let's see if we can outrun the law' and we did".

He made arrangements to make the trip in a more organised manner on Friday, September 30. The party would consist of Bill Hickman, Rolf Wutherich and Sanford Roth. Roth was a professional photographer in his 40s, Jimmy had become friendly with him and Mrs Roth during the making of *Giant*, he intended later to produce a book on his coming travels in Europe, Jimmy was to write the book and Roth, who knew Europe well, would pick the locations and take the photos. Jimmy had also purchased, about a year before, a second-hand Ford station wagon, just for general use. He hired a trailer to carry the Porsche and planned to drive to Salinas with the Porsche on the trailer being towed by the big Ford, with all four taking turns at driving. It would be a long, slow but happy trip.

Absorbed in Anguish
© Mike Shaw

Much Bridled Beauty
© Mike Shaw

Natalie Wood
© Mike Shaw

Bright-Light Window

© Mike Shaw

Part IV

The Crash and After

Jimmy's last day on earth, Friday, September 30, 1955, began at 8 am at Competition Motors where he met Rolf, who took the Porsche into the main workshop and gave it a thorough check-over, plus new plugs, he also fixed a seat belt to the driver's side, but not on the passenger's side because as a track car it would carry only one person when racing. He also fixed a small 8-inch plastic racing windscreen, just to give some protection against wind at very high speed. Jimmy painted on his racing number, 130, and also painted on his nickname for the car, "The Little Bastard". By 11.45 am Rolf had finished on the car and then split for home to get cleaned up and changed. At 12.30 pm Jimmy's father and Uncle Charlie stopped by to say "All the best with the race". Jimmy invited them along, but they declined as Charlie was returning home and neither men were into car racing anyway, but they had lunch together at a cafeteria on Vine Street at the Hollywood Ranch Market, a short distance from 'Competition Motors'.

Winton Dean said later about his son, "I saw him on that last day, he was looking good and in high spirits, he had everything going for him that's why I'll never go for the suicide theory. I know too that we parted friends". Just before 2 pm the Ford complete with trailer and Porsche in tow, pulled up outside Sanford Roth's place, Bill Hickman was also there. Sanford's wife made a quick round of coffees for all, except Jimmy who had his favourite drink, milk. The four men were now in a very happy frame of mind. Bill put a shot of whisky in his own coffee and Jimmy putting on the voice of a mid-West preacher, warned him about the dangers of alcohol. Jim was himself virtually tee-total. The weather was perfect, warm and sunny with a slight breeze. As they left the house, Jimmy said, "With a day like this who wants to be shut in that big old bus", meaning the Ford, and with that he started to unload the Porsche.

Rolf had misgivings about this, he pointed out that it was a track, not a road car, but Jimmy said it could do with the extra mileage as it still had under 700 miles on the speedo. So away the little party went, Jimmy driving the Porsche, Rolf as passenger. Sanford driving the Ford, pulling the now empty trailer, with Bill for company – plus all luggage and racing gear. As they headed out of LA on the long winding freeways they kept each other in sight, sometimes the Ford leading, doing around 65 miles per hour – the speed limit for that part of the road at that time was 55 miles per hour – with the Porsche ambling along at something like a third of its potential speed.

At around 3 o'clock they made a stop at a roadside snack bar, mainly because Rolf wanted to check over the engine. This he did and decided everything was perfect, even the oil pressure was just right, something he paid particular attention to with this type of machine on its first long run. While Rolf attended to his work the other men chatted and joked and also made plans to spend a couple of days in San Francisco after the races, instead of returning to LA.

"OK", said Rolf, "she's ticking like a clock". "Let's go", said Jimmy. He clipped a pair of dark lenses over his ordinary glasses, put his red nylon jacket behind the seat as the sun was now getting very warm. Rolf recalls that after being on the road again for about 15 minutes they were flagged down by a speed cop, Officer O.V. Hunter. and both Jimmy and Sanford were given speeding tickets for doing 70 miles per hour in a 45 miles per hour zone. The policeman, after giving the tickets, asked them questions about the car. "I've never seen anything quite like it before, it looked like a silver torpedo, he said. Jimmy told him, jokingly "I can't get it to run properly under 80 miles per hour".

Sanford told Jimmy to "ease up" because he kept losing sight of him. "See you for dinner in Paso Robles, about 175 miles further on", replied Jimmy. They drove on, passing through small towns like Formosa and Lost Hills, then on to Route 466 (nowadays it's Route 46). They came to Blackwell's Corner about 5 pm just a small gathering of buildings either side of the road. Jimmy slowed to around 40 miles per hour and noticed outside one store a grey Mercedes 300 SL. He pulled over at once. "Let's stretch our legs", he said to Rolf.

He looked over the Mercedes for a while until Sanford and Bill caught up. Sanford bought some fruit for the road, giving Jimmy an apple. Jimmy was talking to the young owner of the S L 300, "What do you do to have a car like this", Jimmy asked rather bluntly. It turned out that the 21-year-old lad was Lance Revson, the son of Barbara Hutton who owned Woolworth Stores throughout the world. On learning this Jimmy cut short the conversation, his strong dislike of people who had inherited wealth returning, he made a remark to the effect that he had to get every penny together himself, to buy his Porsche. Taking a big bite of the apple he climbed back into "The Little Bastard". The sun was now losing a little of its glare. so he unclipped the dark lenses from his glasses, then leaving his seat belt undone, he set off for the last leg – not only of this journey, but of his journey through life.

The long flat road stretched out in front of them, hardly any other traffic, only the station wagon way behind and rapidly disappearing in Jimmy's rear view mirror

The countryside was now mainly desert either side of the road, stretching to the horizon. The sun was directly in front of them, shining in their eyes, but it was setting fast now, another hour or so and it would be twilight, almost dark. The air that rushed past their heads was still very warm, Jimmy wore his white T-shirt, Rolf a red one. At the start Rolf had been somewhat overawed by the fact that he was travelling with a film star, but by now the two had become pals, Jimmy never talking about films unless he was asked and as a film fan Rolf did ask Jimmy about people like Liz Taylor and other famous people, he told Rolf that Liz was a great girl to work with. "One of the best", he said. He also said he hoped to work again with Nick Ray, who directed "Rebel". "That man's a great human being, not like some of the bastards I've met in this town", he added. He also chatted about farming and his mother.

"Man, I wish she'd lived to see all this", he said. "You know, she would only be 46 now". Stunned by the poignancy of his last remark Jimmy lapsed into silence. Rolf, unable to think of a suitable reply, quietly closed his eyes and listened to the steady drone of the engine. At times on this long stretch of empty road, Jimmy took the car to over 100 miles per hour, then dropped down to 70 miles per hour. As he approached the tiny town of Cholame (pronounced Shalom) Jimmy noticed a car way up ahead coming towards him. It was a 1951 model Ford Tudor (not a Plymouth as was widely reported). It had a white body and a black roof and stopped in the middle of the road, its front wheels on the centre line, waiting to turn across Jimmy's path into Road Number 41.

As the big Ford was slowly inching forward Jimmy slowed his speed to around 50 miles per hour. Jimmy's last half-questioning remark to the sleepy Rolf was, "That guy up there has got to stop, he's seen us", with that the Ford pulled right across the road. As Rolf described it later, the Ford suddenly lurched forward. Jimmy slammed on the brakes, leaving skid marks in the road of over 30 feet. The impact killed James Dean outright. The steering wheel smashed into his chest and his head was flung back with such force that it broke his neck. The time was 5.50 pm. Rolf was flung 12 feet from the car, suffering fractured jaw, broken hip and legs, multiple cuts and extreme shock. He would spend the next three months in hospital, but would recover in time.

The other driver, Donald Turnupseed, was travelling alone and on his way to Tulare, a small town nearby, to spend the weekend with his parents. His head had gone into and smashed the windscreen, but apart from a badly cut face and shock he was OK. A couple of passing motorists stopped, one drove on to a nearby house and phoned an ambulance, a highway patrol car arrived within a few minutes after getting a message from Cholame on the car radio. They found Jimmy pinned behind the wheel of the almost disintegrated Porsche. The car was off the road and on the wide verge. It had come to a stop against a telegraph pole. Rolf lay still conscious but dumb with shock, nearby. The Ford had ended up at right angles across the highway, its driver's door hanging open, its front end smashed and a hole in the driver's side of the windscreen. The driver, Turnupseed, was staggering around in the road, repeating "I never saw them, I just never saw them". Blood was streaming down his face, the patrolman got him to sit down on the side of the road. Now Sanford and Bill arrived on the scene. "At first I never realised it was any connection with Jimmy", he said, "I just saw this big sedan parked across the road and this young guy running around, bleeding, and Oh my God, I saw the Porsche and Jimmy still in the car, his arm hanging almost casually over the side of the door. Instinctively I began taking pictures, I don't know, I thought they may be needed for insurance reasons or something. Bill ran across to help Jimmy and Rolf, then with sirens wailing and red light flashing a white Buick ambulance arrived. The crew-driver Paul Moreno and assistant, Collier Davidson, pulled in alongside the Porsche. As carefully as they could they lifted Jimmy out of the car and on to a stretcher and in to the ambulance, then did the same for Rolf, sliding him into the berth above Jimmy, then they took off at speed for the Paso Robles War Memorial Hospital.

The crew kept Jimmy on oxygen during the journey, but on arrival a doctor climbed into the ambulance and checked Jimmy for signs of life, there were none. So Jimmy was now officially dead. Later driver Moreno said, "I knew he was dead when we got him out of the crumpled sports car".

Four days later it was Winton's turn to travel with a dead relative from California to Indiana. This time by plane. The body lay in state for three days at the Hunt's Funeral Parlour, the same firm that dealt with his mother's funeral, also the same store where a year before Jimmy had posed in one of the coffins and got a photographer to take photos for Life magazine, who, by the way, refused to print them.

On Saturday, October 8, 1955, an orderly crowd of around 2,000 people turned up to see Jimmy laid to rest. The service was held at Fairmont Friends Church, by the friend of his youth, the Rev. James De-Weerd, he quoted from the Bible:

"Whereas ye know not what shall be the morrow, for what is your life? It is even a vapour that appeareth for a little time and then vanish away".

After the service the procession of cars drove down Main Street and out a short distance to the Park Cemetery, once an old Indian burial ground. Jimmy's coffin was carried by six of his old school friends. The grave lies on a slight ridge open to the Indiana wind and rain. Jimmy was now not only at peace, but had finally come home.

Three days after the funeral, a Coroner's jury listened to details of the accident. First the two highway patrol officers who were first on the scene, then Officer Hunter who gave Jimmy a speeding ticket earlier in the day, then two men who watched the Porsche go by just before the crash. They swore that

Wutherich was driving "The man in the red T-shirt", they said. Wutherich, in a written report from his hospital bed, completely denied this, he pointed out that the driver's seat took the full force of the impact and if he had been driving he would not have survived.

Some jury members thought it strange that he had not had a turn at driving on such a long trip, after all he was a Porsche factory-trained mechanic, so there could have been no question in Jimmy's mind as to whether he could handle the car properly. Many other witnesses were called, bystanders, ambulance men, etc. Lastly, Donald Turnupseed, he stayed with the same story he had told the highway patrol at the time, he just never saw the other car. He said he was still at college and was driving home for the weekend, he had to take a left hand fork at the Y intersection, as he came around the long curve in the road he stopped, looked up the main road towards Bakersfield, saw nothing and started to cross into the smaller road towards Tulare, then smash! "I just didn't know what hit me", he said.

The police worked out by re-checking the distance of Jimmy's route and taking out the time for stops that his average speed over the last 2½ hours that day was an incredible 86 miles per hour, therefore, if correct, he must have been doing well over

100 miles per hour on many of the long, straight sections of the road. They jury wanted the police or Mr Turnupseed to explain how he could not have seen the Porsche. Reasons or theories put forward by Highway Patrol were the silver colour of the Porsche, blending with the road in the slightly fading light, and the extremely low profile of the car which from Turnupseed's position looking straight ahead would all make Jimmy's car very hard to see. The jury were out for 20 minutes, then returned a verdict of accidental death and that no charges were to be made against Mr Turnupseed. The coroner, Mr Merrick, then closed the case.

At the time of the crash Sandford Roth took pictures of Jimmy laying dead at the wheel of his car, these photos would, of course, answer a lot of questions that arise. Who was driving? Did Jimmy still have his glasses on? Was his seat belt still left undone? etc. But Sanford refused to release these pictures to anyone. Some people doubt their existence. I feel such photos were taken, we publish here shots of Jimmy being taken to the ambulance, so it's reasonable to assume that they existed, but maybe Sanford destroyed them. He was offered huge sums by a German newspaper in the late '50s, and let's face it, photographers like most other people do have their price. After Sanford's death in 1965, his wife Beaulah denied all knowledge of them, so the question remains unanswered.

My last call after visiting Fairmount was a long bus ride north to Detroit to see a Mr Miller, alias "Moondog". Jimmy's street-singing pal. I located him in a rather run-down section of town. I climbed the concrete stairs to his flat, a weary-looking coloured woman opened the door. I explained about my earlier phone call and she showed me to an upper room. She turned out to be Moondog's married daughter, with whom the old man now lived. He greeted me warmly, he had a large but bleak room, furnished with a bed, table and a couple of chairs. He recalled his singing days with Jimmy "We had some laughs, man". His conversation was dotted with quotations from Shakespeare and the poets, something he had in common with Jimmy. He took great pleasure in showing me his collection of books and a couple of signed photos that Jimmy had given him. "You know, he wanted me to go out to Hollywood and make a musical with him", the old man laughed until tears filled his eyes, "Ever hear of anything so crazy?", he asked, "I ain't never been out West and I've no wish to go, but I would like to be back in New York with Jimmy, especially in 1951 or '52, those were great years. I only have 15% of my vision, so I've never really seen him on the screen, but I can tell by the soundtrack that he was good, I'm glad he made it. You tell me he's buried near his mother, I'm pleased about that. Yes Sir. I'll tell you something else, if he were alive today he wouldn't let old Moondog be living like this". he gestured his hands around the room.

It was easy to see that he was not a well man, and a couple of hours and several coffees laced with whisky later, he insisted on walking with me to the bus station. He seemed pleased to have an excuse to get out of the house. "You know", said Moondog, "for a short time, Jimmy made life for a lot of folk more entertaining, more interesting, maybe more bearable, and Jimmy's personal path was steep and rugged. Yet he went far and fast in a very short time, from farm boy to racing driver and movie star.

"When he died he left almost no personal possessions, just things like bongo drums and paintings that he did while living in New York, and a lock of his mother's hair, that he kept all those years. You'd expect a movie star to leave a lot more, but he was not the sort of guy to own anything. There was one poem he was always quoting when we were together, and it still reminds me of him, because he liked it so much.

As I shook hands with him, and began boarding my bus, I asked if he could remember how it went. He quoted me a few lines that I hurriedly wrote down. He waved as the bus pulled away. I knew with his poor eyesight he could no longer see the bus, but I waved back until the dignified old man blurred into the background. On my return to London I traced the poem reproduced here in full ...

"Let me five out my years in heat of blood!
Let me die drunken with the dreamer's wine!
Let me not see this soul-house built of mud
Go toppling to the dust – a vacant shrine!
Let me go quickly like a candle light
Snuffed out just at the heyday of its glow!
Give me high noon – and let it then be night!
Thus would I go.
And grant me, when I face the grisly Thing,
One haughty cry to pierce the gray Perhaps!
0 let me be a tune-swept fiddlestring
That feels the Master Melody – and snaps."

"Master Meldoy" attributed to 20th century American poet John G Neihardt.

Moondog was right for James Dean, that's ... the way it was.

Lone-Star State
© Mike Shaw

Land-Locked Submariner
© Mike Shaw

Serenity Under Seige
© Mike Shaw

Banquet For One
© Mike Shaw

Chapter V

The Turnupseed/Moretti Interview

I know Maria to be a respected American writer and journalist with an incisive style and I feel proud that she has given Stagedoor Publications permission to let her interview appear for the first time as part of my book. When I listened to it on cassette questions that had puzzled me for years were at last answered. Why on such a long drive did Weutherich not take a turn at driving? Why did so many witnesses say that Weutherich was at the wheel when the Porsche went past them?

An American TV show called 'What Happened' did a computer re-enactment of the crash. It showed that the Porsche was going no more than 50mph (normal driving speed). I've long had my doubts about if Jim was driving and now after all this time my questions have been answered. The thing that stays with me is the sadness in Turnupseeds voice as he at last puts the story straight, but then the James Dean story is one that never goes away.

Terry Cunningham. (London. 2004)

The Moretti Interview

Hi, this is Maria Moretti talking to you from Southern California. Today we are going to discuss an event that happened long, long ago. To be exact, it was the 30th September 1955 at around 5.45 in the evening when movie idol James Dean was killed in a car crash. To say Dean has become a cult figure is the understatement of all time. His face and his films are known in every part of the world. How many presidents has our Country had since 1955 and how many of their names can you recall? That's right, not too many, but Jimmy Dean is still super famous. His face can be seen adorning everything from T-shirts to coffee mugs and posters etc. Before coming here today I asked over 30 people who were not even around in 1955 how they thought Jimmy Dean had died. They all knew he had died in a Californian head on car crash. Some of them knew that he was driving a sports car and was speeding and they generally thought that it was Jimmy Dean's fault. Not one of them knew who or what Jim, had crashed into. Well that's the point of this interview this afternoon. The man that Jim did crash into had the strange name of Donald Gene Turnupseed. He has never given an interview or told his side of the story since that sad day in 1955, but he's here now to talk to me about it. Welcome Donald.

Donald

Hi Maria.

Maria

Don, why have you decided to talk about the crash after this long, long time?

Donald

Well lots of reasons. I am getting to be an old man. My health is not as good as it could be, so I just want to put the record straight. This is basically, what I wanted to say at the inquest. I said that I did not see Mr. Dean's car until it struck mine. That's not true. I did see him approaching me. He was going fast, maybe too fast. Some witnesses said he was doing about 80 mph. That's bullshit. I'd say when his car hit me he was moving at around 35mph. The accident was both our faults. We misjudged each other. I blame the driver not hitting the brakes and for reacting far too slowly. I blame my misjudging my turn and then panicking.

Maria

So you did see him coming towards you?

Donald

Yeah, you see Maria I was going along listening to music on my radio; there was this station that played all the hit records at the time. You know Doris Day, Kay Starr. Then I realised I was coming up to my turnoff at junction 41. I saw a sports car in the distance and I thought I had plenty of time to turn. Then like an idiot I changed my mind. Maybe the music was distracting me because I said to myself "Oh he's not moving that fast and decided to turn. I don't know, maybe they slowed as they approached me because then it was like in slow motion and I could see the two guys in the car. The one in the red shirt was driving. I have asked myself a million times, why the hell didn't he hit those brakes. The other guy threw his arms up over his face. Then there was this awful smash and the sound of metal twisting.

Maria

So you are going along a little too fast listening to the radio, you hit the brakes for your turn off, you see a sports car coming towards you in the other lane, so you pulled back, then think maybe I can make it and you pull across the road and the Dean car hits you.

Donald

That's it. I left 30 ft skid marks in Dean's lane.

Maria

Tell me, where were you going to on that historic day?

Donald

Well at that time, the time of the crash that is I was 23 years old, I had enlisted in the navy when I was only 20 and served in Korea but now I wanted to join my father in his Engineering business, so to study Electrical Engineering, I enrolled as a freshman at the Cal-Poly. That's the Californian Polytechnic Institute in San Luis Obispo. That's down on the coast around 100 miles from my parents home in Tulare. So at weekends I'd go back to enjoy some home cooking and that's where I was going. I have read reports that said, it was almost dark. It wasn't. There was still plenty of daylight. The sun was to my left and still bright. I overtook a slow moving big car as I passed through the town of Shandon on highway 466 at around 5.30pm. Up to the crash it had been an uneventful journey.

Maria

What sort of car did you have Don?

Donald

It was a Ford Tudor, a 1950 model and it had a black and white paint job that made it look like a police car and I'd just fitted white wall tyres. I was young and brash and often cars would slow down for me, thinking that I was a police patrol car. Maybe I had gotten used to that and subconsciously thought that the Dean car would slow down for me to let me across.

Maria

Don't you think, Don, that by staying quiet all these years has maybe made you appear guilty, almost as though you had something to hide.

Donald

Yeah, I agree. It was a mistake not to come out in the open from the start. I guess all that I have told you about the crash was what I had to hide, but at the time I was scared, real scared. The hate mail I got back then was just unbelievable. The fans made my life a nightmare. I got threatening phones calls day and night. It went on for years. In the end I had a complete breakdown, so to get away from it all I re-enlisted in the Navy until 1960.

Maria

Tell me more about who you thought was driving the other car, the sports car?

Donald

It was no sports car. It was a German Porsche racing car. Mr. Dean was on his way to a car race that he was going to take part in with that car. It was silver and real low slung. Looked kinda like a torpedo on wheels. The other guy, Rolf Weutherich, was older than Dean. He was German and he worked for the Porsche car company. Now I had never heard of James Dean. At that time only one of his movies had been released and I hadn't seen it, but he wore a white shirt that day and it was the man in the red shirt who was driving and he was flung clear out of the car.

Maria

Tell me about the scene of the crash?

Donald

Well I was more hurt than the papers reported, my nose was broken and I had cracked ribs and I was shocked and stunned. I walked around in a daze. You know I sat around without treatment, waiting for cars to be towed away, then the police just got into their cars and left me standing there on the dark road. I hitched a lift in the end, but by the time I got hospital treatment 5 hours had passed since the .accident, but you were asking about the crash. Well a couple of cars pulled up to see if they could help. One guy was a Tom Frederick. He swore that the Porsche had overtaken them back down the highway going very fast and that Weutherich was driving. Another man who stopped was Don Dooley. He also said that Weutherich was at the wheel and they both swore this at the inquest. A patrolman, Ron Nelson, arrived who treated me badly, started abusing me, saying it was my fault. He made me breath out so he could smell my breath to see if I had been drinking, but I'd had no drink. Even at the inquest he insinuated that I was to blame. At the same time, a couple of friends of Mr. Dean who were going to the race meeting with him pulled up in a big Ford towing a trailer for the Porsche. One was a guy called Sandford Roth, a photographer, and he started taking pictures, while the other man, a Bill Hickman, now he ran over to Mr. Dean and held him in his arms, then he saw the other guy taking pictures. I remember he screamed "You no good son of a bitch, I am an ex marine and I'll smash your skull with that camera".

Maria
Was Jimmy Dean alive?

Donald

Yes he was. I was too scared to go near the car. I was maybe 15 ft away, but Hickman was saying something like "Hang on old son, hang on old buddy". Then he walked away from the car and went up to the photographer and I heard him say, "He's gone, Jimmy's gone". The other guy just said "Oh my God". Hickman then asked who Mildred was and that Mr. Roth replied that was the name of Jimmy's mother. "Well" said Hickman "Jim said her name, then said thanks Bill, but I gotta go home now". Then this Hickman guy walked over to me. I thought he was going to say something, but when he got close he gave me one hell of a punch in the guts. It was like being hit by a train. I just sank to my knees and rolled over, so winded that I couldn't even speak and that lousy patrolman just looked the other way. That Hickman was a stunt driver for the movies. Do you recall that Steve McQueen movie, Bullet.

Maria

Yes I've seen it on TV, they have that car chase flying up and down those steep hills in San Francisco.

Donald

Yeah, well Hickman was driving that car Steve McQueen was chasing.

Maria

You must have enjoyed seeing how the chase ended, they hit a gas station and got blown away in a ball of flame, right? But in the end Don, you were cleared of any blame?

Donald

Yes the inquest cleared me of any blame, it was purely and simply an accident, but Weutherich and his insurance company sued me for dangerous driving. Then a couple of months after the inquest I got a letter from Weutherich asking if I would visit him in the War Memorial Hospital at Paso Robles. I was in two minds what to do. Well I told no one about it, but I set off to see him. When I went into his room I was shocked. His legs were in plaster and his jaw was broken and was wired up so he could only speak very slowly, one word at a time. That was bad enough but his English was very poor and he spoke with a real heavy German accent. Some of the time he wrote what he wanted to say on a writing pad.

Maria

What did he want to say?

Donald

Well he came straight out with it. He said "You know I was

driving and I know the crash was your fault. Now we are both in a very dangerous situation, we could become known as the men who killed James Dean and Jimmy is about the most famous face on earth right now and he has a fanatical following of fans all over the world. How long would it be before both of us were gunned down by some lunatic fan". I remember I tried to make a silly joke and told him that as he was pinned down in a hospital, they would get him within the hour and me sometime within the next 24 hours, so I agreed that what he said made sense. He told me Jim would not want our lives destroyed because he died in a car crash, so we made a pact to keep quiet, a pact that we both kept until today. He dropped the insurance case against me and I never saw or heard from him again. He died in a crash himself back in Germany in 1981. He was driving way too fast, but this time he was alone and no one else was involved. You know he had a very bad record for dangerous driving even before the crash. He had been involved in several accidents both here and in Germany.

Maria
So Jimmy died because of the bad or dangerous driving of both you and Weutherich and through no fault of his own, right?

Donald

That's about it Maria.

Maria

I feel sorry for you Don, one car accident pretty much destroyed your life.

Donald

There's not been a day since the crash that I have not thought about it. I have never been allowed to. Jimmy Dean's face stares out at me from everywhere, magazines, newspapers, TV, the after effects of that crash ruined my young life. Hate mail, phone calls, being abused in the street, why even a few months back a guy pulled over on a Harley Davidson motor cycle came over to my car and punched me in the face through the open window and said that's for Jim.

Maria

Did you punch back?

Donald

No, over a lifetime of this type of thing, I've learnt not to. You see, if it had been any other famous movie star of that time that had died in the crash, say Gary Cooper or Clark Gable, I would not have gone through all this hell. They were loved by the public sure, but Dean fans are a special type. I don't know if they admire his movies or his acting style, they just worship the man himself and I gotta say that among Dean fans you get a large share of weirdoes and crazies. It used to get me so low at times that I wished that I had died in the crash myself, but I have tried to lead a decent life and after all's said and done, it was just a sad accident.

Maria
It sure was Don, and all true James Dean fans know that. I want to thank you for having the courage to talk to me about it. I am sure I speak for everyone when I say I wish you well and all our readers out there and Dean fans everywhere will respect you and your privacy.

Donald
Thank you Maria. My best wishes to you all.

© Maria Moretti

On Mr Turnupseed's instructions this interview was not to be released during his lifetime. He died eight months after recording it. Apart from being played on one USA radio station this is the first time it has been published.

Chapter VI

The Things They Said

You would have thought that a boy being gone all these years would leave us in peace, but on Jimmy's birthday last year I looked out the window and counted over a dozen cars parked outside the gate, people just looking at the house.
Marcus Winslow, Jimmy's Uncle

His death caused a loss in the movie world that our industry could ill afford, had he lived long enough I feel he would have made some incredible films; he had sensitivity and a capacity to express emotion.
Gary Cooper, Film Star

I remember one cold winter's day we'd been making music out on the streets for hours; me on guitar, Jimmy on bongos. We'd made about two dollars each, I said, "Let's split and get some food". I spent mine on hot coffee, he spent his on seeing a movie.
Moondog, New York Street Singer

I always had the feeling there was in Jimmy a sort of doomed quality.
Lee Strasberg, Director of the Actors' Studio, New York

He was desperately lonely and had many inward problems so it was hard to get close to him, he was a strange and sensitive character with tremendous imagination.
Julie Harris, Actress

When I worked with him on TV I found him to be an intelligent young actor who seemed to live only for his work, he was completely dedicated and although a shy person he could hold a good conversation on many wide-ranging subjects.
Ronald Reagan, Film Actor (later President of the United States)

Even today at odd times I find myself thinking of Jimmy and how much he helped us all. He often comes in to my mind that way. A while back I was out West filming, so I took a look around the "Rebel" location, the tears just flowed, I had to get away fast.
Sal Mineo, Film Actor

He was pure gold, the images he created on screen in his three films are as contemporary today as they were when they were made. He was one of the greatest actors that ever lived.
Dennis Hooper, Film Actor/Director

I think Dean died at the right time, had he lived he would never have been able to keep up with all that publicity.
Humphrey Bogart, Film Star

Rock on, Jimmy Dean, your public are still with you. Right now in some small mid-West town, a Greyhound's ride from nowhere, you're still up there on screen, spelling out the message of lonely, human isolation.
Terry Cunningham, Writer

The guy was guided by some inner light of his own, maybe even he did not know what it was. I knew he had been motherless since early childhood and he missed a lot of love, I think he was still waiting for some lost tenderness.
George Stevens, Film Director

The whole time I worked with the man I never got a civil word out of him. He always seemed resentful about something.
Rock Hudson, Film Star

Anyone who came into contact with Jimmy found that their lives were never quite the same again. God knows where a spirit like that comes from, they flash across our lives like shooting stars.
Elizabeth Taylor, Film Star

I know by heart all the dialogue of James Dean's films. I could watch "Rebel" a hundred times over
Elvis Presley, Singer

That man knew where it was at, he was rocking.
Mick Jagger, The Rolling Stones

When we first worked together we became close friends, but as time went on he became more neurotic, he turned against me, he was a very troubled person.
Elia Kazan, Film Director

You know when you see a bird in a cage, how you want to open the cage door and say "fly bird". Well that's the way I always felt when I was with him.
Jimmy's teenage girlfriend, Fairmount, Indiana

If he were alive today he'd be working on a stage., he'd want no part of the mind-numbing garbage that cinema and TV turn out these days.

Nick Ray, Film Director

When we started out there were five Beatles, the fifth one, a guy called Stewart Sutcliffe, he was really our leader, and he was really into the James Dean thing, he idolised him. Stewart died young before we made the big time, but I suppose you could say that without Jimmy Dean the Beatles would never have existed.

John Lennon, The Beatles

Stewart Sutcliffe, the fifth Beatle died aged 21 from a brain tumour, just a few weeks before the group made their first hit record ("Love Me Do") in 1962. Fans say he was the founder of the whole Beatles sound. He was obsessed with the Dean cult. He copied Dean in everything, clothes mannerisms, speech, etc. He was the ultimate fan.

Credits

Plays

1952

WOMAN OF TRACHIS – (off Broadway)

THE METAMORPHOSIS – (off Broadway; dramatic reading)

SEE THE JAGUAR with Constance Ford, Arthur Kennedy

1954

THE IMMORALIST with Geraldine Page, Louis Jourdan

Films

1951

FIXED BAYONETS – 20th Century-Fox, with Richard Basehart, Gene Evans

1952

HAS ANYBODY SEEN MY GAL-Universal-International, with Charles Coburn, Piper Laurie, Lynn Bari, Rock Hudson

1954

*EAST OF EDEN – Warner Bros., with Julie Harris, Raymond Massey, Jo Van Fleet, Burl Ives
*Dean was nominated for an Academy Award as Best Actor

1955

REBEL WITHOUT A CAUSE – Warner Bros., with Natalie Wood, Sal Mineo.

1956

*GIANT – George Stevens – Warner Bros., with Elizabeth Taylor, Rock Hudson, Sal Mineo, Carroll Baker
*Dean was nominated for an Academy Award as Best Actor
THE JAMES DEAN STORY – Warner Bros. Documentary

Television

1950

Father Peyton's TV Theatre. "Hill Number One"

1952

US Steel Hour: "Prologue to Glory"

1953

Kate Smith Hour: "Hound of Heaven"

Treasury Men in Action: "The Case of the Watchful Dog"

Danger: "No Room"

Treasury Men in Action: "The Case of the Sawed-Off Shotgun"

Campbell Sound Stage: "Something for an Empty Briefcase"

Studio One Summer Theatre: "Sentence of Death"

Danger: "Death Is My Neighbour"

"The Big Story"

"Omnibus" (film clips of legit shows)

Kraft TV Theatre: "Keep Our Honor Bright"

Campbell Sound Stage: "A Long Time Till Dawn"

Armstrong Circle Theatre: "The Bells of Cockaigne"

Johnson's Wax Program: "Robert Montgomery Presents Harvest"

1954

Danger: "Padlocks"

General Electric Theatre: "The Dark, Dark Hours"

General Electric Theatre: "I'm a Fool"

1955

US Steel Hour: "The Thief"

Lever Brothers' Lux Video Theatre: "The Life of Emile Zola", followed by an interview with James Dean

Schlitz Playhouse: "The Unlighted Road"

1956

Philco TV Playhouse: "Run Like A Thief"

Awards

1954

Theatre World Award as "Most Promising Newcomer" for his performance in THE IMMORALIST

1955

PHOTOPLAY GOLD MEDAL AWARD given posthumously for his "outstanding dramatic appearances"

Award presented by MODERN SCREEN magazine, in honour of its 25th anniversary Presented on Colgate Variety Hour

Printed in the United Kingdom
by Lightning Source UK Ltd.
102664UKS00001B/272